The Liberal Heart of Europe

Francesco Giavazzi
Francesco Lefebvre D'Ovidio
Alberto Mingardi
Editors

The Liberal Heart of Europe

Essays in Memory of Alberto Giovannini

palgrave
macmillan

Editors
Francesco Giavazzi
IGIER
Bocconi University
Milan, Italy

Francesco Lefebvre D'Ovidio
Sapienza University of Rome
Rome, Italy

Alberto Mingardi
IULM University
Milan, Italy

Bruno Leoni Institute
Milan, Italy

ISBN 978-3-030-60367-0 ISBN 978-3-030-60368-7 (eBook)
https://doi.org/10.1007/978-3-030-60368-7

This Palgrave Macmillan imprint is published by the registered company Springer Nature Switzerland AG.
The registered company address is: Gewerbestrasse 11, 6330 Cham, Switzerland

Acknowledgments

This book is largely composed of the proceedings of a conference organized in Turin on March 15 and 16, 2019. That conference was the brainchild of Alberto Giovannini and the present editors, but it was organized in practice by Istituto Bruno Leoni and the Centro Studi sul Federalismo (CSF). We are grateful for the support of Flavio Brugnoli and Alfonso Iozzo, from CSF, and for the splendid work of the Istituto Bruno Leoni's team. The conference was sponsored by the Atlas Economic Network, the Compagnia di San Paolo, and the Zampa Foundation, that we thank profoundly.

Last but not least, we want to acknowledge the outstanding work of Veronica Cancelliere, who brilliantly helped us as an editorial assistant in putting this book together.

The Liberal Heart of Europe is of course dedicated to the memory of Alberto Giovannini, who is sorely missed.

Contents

Notes on Contributors

Edmond Alphandéry is the founder and Chairman of the Euro 50 Group which gathers leading European personalities concerned with monetary policy of the European Central Bank. He launched in 2018 the "Task Force on Carbon Pricing in Europe", a group of personalities coming from various countries of the European Union to promote carbon pricing in Europe to fight climate change. Edmond Alphandéry is a Senior Advisor of Banque Nomura France, Advisor for Quadrille Capital, Member of the Advisory Board of Montrose, and Vice President of the Club of Three. From 1993–1995 he worked as a Minister of the Economy of France. From 1998 to 2012, he served as Chairman of CNP Assurances, and prior to this appointment, he was Chairman of Electricité de France (EDF). From 2010 to May 2019, he was a Board member of ENGIE and the President of its Strategic Committee. Edmond Alphandéry is the author of numerous articles and books devoted to economic and monetary affairs.

Leszek H. Balcerowicz born in 1947, he is an economist, professor at the Warsaw School of Economics, and an MBA graduate of St. John's University in New York. He is the author of the economic reforms in post-communist Poland after 1989; Deputy Prime Minister and Minister of Finance in the first non-communist government of Poland after World War II (1989–1991) and then again from 1997 to 2000; President of the National Bank of Poland (2001–2007); and laureate of over 30 honorary doctorates from universities all around the world. He is also laureate of many prestigious Polish and international prizes and distinctions including Friedrich Hayek's and Milton Friedman Prize, and the Order of White Eagle—the highest Polish decoration. In 2007 Leszek Balcerowicz founded The Civil Development Forum Foundation—FOR, a think tank based in Warsaw, that promotes the rule of law and economic freedom. Since then he has been serving as the Chairman of its Council. He belongs to certain international associations including The Group of Thirty and Mont Pelerin Society.

Agnès Bénassy-Quéré is Professor of Economics at University of Paris 1 Panthéon-Sorbonne and Paris School of Economics. She is a former Member of the French macroprudential authority, the tax advisory council, the productivity council, the Franco-German council of economic experts, and the Banque of France general board. She is also a former non-resident fellow at Bruegel and a member of the CESIfo network. From 2012 until 2017, she chaired the French Council of Economic Advisors. Prior positions include Director of CEPII, the French research institute in international economics (2006–2012), and academic positions at École Polytechnique, the University of Paris-Ouest and the University of Lille 2. Her research interests focus on the international monetary system and European macroeconomic policy.

Michael C. Burda is an American macroeconomist and professor at the Humboldt University of Berlin, and he received his BA, MA, and PhD (1987) at Harvard University. He has served as director of the Humboldt's Institute for Economic Theory II since 1993, and he has also taught at Berkeley, INSEAD, and the European School of Management and Technology (ESMT). In 1998, Burda received the Gossen Prize of the German Verein für Socialpolitik, and holds an honorary doctorate from the Otto-von-Guericke-Universität Magdeburg. He is a research fellow at the Centre for Economic Policy Research (CEPR), Program Director at the Institute for the Study of Labor (IZA), and a Fellow of the European Economic Association. His research is primarily in macroeconomics, labor economics, and issues of European integration.

Francesco Giavazzi is Full Professor of Economics and vice chair of university's Advisory Council and was deputy rector (2000–2002). He is also a visiting professor at Massachusetts Institute of Technology (MIT; 2003–2013). He graduated in electrical engineering (Politecnico di Milano, 1972) and holds a PhD in Economics (MIT, 1978). He is CEPR research fellow and former trustee, NBER research associate, Scientific Committee Chair (CEPII, Paris) and Bellagio Group member. In 1991, he contributed to founding IGIER (an economics research institute jointly created by NBER, CEPR and Bocconi University), serving as first director and president to 2002. He was deputy director general of the Italian Treasury, 1991–1994, and spending review adviser to the Italian government in 2012 and to the Federal Reserve Bank of New York in 2013, 2015, and 2016. He has been also part of the Group of Economic Advisers to the Italian Prime Minister, 1998–2000, and of the Group of Economic Advisers to the President of the European Commission, 2000–2010. He was a Houblon-Norman Fellow (Bank of England) in 2002, member of the External Evaluation Committee of IMF Research Activities, 1999, and member of the Riksbank Evaluation for the Swedish Parliament, 2006. His publications include the following: *Limiting Exchange Rate Flexibility* (with Alberto Giovannini, Cambridge, MA: MIT Press 1989); *The Future of Europe: Reform or Decline.* (with Alberto Alesina, Cambridge, MA: MIT Press 2003); *Austerity: When It Works and When It Doesn't* (with Alberto Alesina and Carlo Favero, Princeton, NJ: Princeton University Press 2019, awarded with the 2019 Hayek Book Prize). For recent writings, please visit: http://didattica.unibocconi.eu/myigier/index.php?IdUte=48751

John R. Gillingham III is a University of Missouri Board of Curators Professor and was Professor of History there until 2007. He received his BA, MA, and PhD (1973) at the University of California, Berkeley, and he is a former Fellow of Harvard University. He was also the Director of the Truman Era Research Program for ten years (1987–1997), and he was research associate at the Institut für Zeitgeschichte in Munich, (1985) and visiting professor at the European University Institute in Florence. He is also a former fellow of the Harvard Center for European Studies, as well as a senior researcher at the Harvard Ukrainian Research Institute. He has authored books on European integration, heavy industry in the Third Reich and the economy of Belgium under Nazi occupation. Gillingham is listed in Marquis' *Who's Who in America* and has received numerous awards and recognitions. His area of expertise covers Political Economy, the European Union, the Trade Agreement Parity (TAP), and the Transatlantic Trade & Investment Partnership (TTIP).

Alberto Giovannini This book is dedicated to Alberto Giovannini (1955–2019), a brilliant economist and dear friend.

Otmar Issing is a German economist who has been serving as President of the Center for Financial Studies since 2006. Issing studied Latin and Greek before he moved to economics at the University of Würzburg from where he received his PhD in 1961 and received the *venia legendi* (1965). In 1967 Issing became director of the Institute for International Economic Relations at the University of Erlangen-Nuremberg and full professor at the faculty of economics and social sciences of the University of Erlangen-Nuremberg. From 1973–1990 he held the chair for money and international economic relations at the University of Würzburg.

From 1988 to 1990 Issing was a member of the German Council of Economic Experts and in 1990 he became a member of the board of the Deutsche Bundesbank with a seat on the Central Bank Council. In 1998 Issing became a member of the Executive Board of the European Central Bank, responsible for the Directorates General Economics and Research as well as its first Chief Economist, and developed the "two pillar" approach to monetary policy decision-making that the ECB has adopted.

Since June 2006 Issing has been president of the Center for Financial Studies (CFS) at the Goethe University in Frankfurt am Main and from 2007 until 2018 he was an international advisor to Goldman Sachs.

In October 2008 appointed by chancellor Merkel Issing chaired an expert group on the new financial order that drew up proposals on how to reform the international financial system (also known as "Issing Commission"). In the years 2008–2010, Issing was also a member of the high-level group of the European Commission on financial supervision in the EU chaired by Jacques de Larosière. He was a Member of the G20 Eminent Persons Group on Global Financial Governance, which was formally established by G20 Finance Ministers and Central Bank Governors for the period 2017–2018.

Stefan Kolev Born 1981 in Sofia, Bulgaria, Stefan Kolev studied economics and business administration at the University of Hamburg. He wrote his PhD thesis at the University of Hamburg on the political economy of neoliberalism. He headed the research project "The Centrally Planned Economy of the GDR—Myth and Reality" at the Hamburg Institute of International Economics HWWI. During his PhD studies Stefan Kolev taught at several universities, including the University of Hamburg, the University of Erfurt, and the Private University of Applied Sciences, Göttingen. He was a guest researcher at the Bulgarian National Bank in 2009 and a visiting scholar at Duke University in 2010.

Since March 2012, Stefan Kolev has been Professor of Political Economy at the University of Applied Sciences Zwickau. He is the deputy director of the Wilhelm Röpke Institute, Erfurt, an advisory board member of the Alliance for the Social Market Economy ASM, Tübingen, and a research fellow of the Hamburg Institute of International Economics HWWI. In 2015 he co-founded the Network for Constitutional Economics and Social Philosophy NOUS, Freiburg. In 2016/2017 he spent six months as a research fellow at the Center for the History of Political Economy at Duke University. In 2019/2020 he spent three months as a visiting scholar at the Ostrom Workshop at Indiana University, Bloomington, and three months as a research fellow at the Center for the History of Political Economy at Duke University. Stefan Kolev has been invited to deliver guest lectures, among others, at Brown University, Roosevelt University Chicago, the University of Basel, the University of Richmond, the University of St. Gallen, and the University of Zurich. He is co-editor of the ORDO Jahrbuch für die Ordnung von Wirtschaft und Gesellschaft and of the Journal of Contextual Economics—Schmollers Jahrbuch.

Stefan Kolev's research focuses on the history of economic thought, especially ordoliberalism, Austrian economics, and the German Historical School, on constitutional political economy, and on economic sociology, especially Max Weber.

Jacques de Larosière entered the French Treasury in 1958 where he worked mostly on international financial matters. From 1974 to 1978 he was Undersecretary for Monetary Affairs. From 1978 to 1987, he was elected Managing Director of the International Monetary Fund (IMF). He was appointed Governor of the Banque de France from 1987 to 1993, and President of the European Bank for Reconstruction and Development (EBRD) from 1993 to 1998. He was also a professor at Sciences PO Paris from 2013 to 2018.

He held the position of Advisor to the Chairman at BNP Paribas from 1998 to 2008, President of the Observatoire de l'Epargne Européenne OEE (1999–2020), Chairman of Eurofi (2000–2017), and Co-Chairman of the "Committee on Crisis Management and Crisis Resolution in Emerging Markets" of the Institute of International Finance, 2003–2009. He was a Trustee of Reuters Founders Share Company Limited (1999–2004), and Member of the Group of Trustees for the Principles for Emerging Markets, 2006. He is the Chairman of the Strategic Committee of the Agence France Trésor, 2004, and Chairman of the Advisory Board of MidEuropa Fund (2006–2018). He was also a Member of the International Advisory Board of China Development Bank (2005–2009) and Member of the Board of Directors of France Telecom (1998–2009). He was a director of the Stichting NYSE Euronext (the Dutch Foundation) and trustee of NYSE Group Trust I (the US Trust) (2007–2014), and he chaired a high-level committee on the reform of the European financial supervisory architecture between Nov. 2008 and Feb. 2009.

He is a Member of the "Académie des Sciences Morales et Politiques" of the Institut de France, Grand Officier of the Legion d'Honneur, KBE, and Member of the French Society of the Cincinnati. He was also awarded with the Grand Croix de l'Ordre du Mérite.

Francesco Lefebvre D'Ovidio is Full Professor of History of International Relations at the Department of Political Science at Università "La Sapienza" in Rome. He is the president of the scientific board at the Italian Ministry of Foreign Affairs for publishing the collection of the *Italian Diplomatic Documents*, and he is a member of the scientific board of the Giulio Andreotti Archive at the Luigi Sturzo Institute in Rome. His latest publications include the following: *L'Italia e il sistema internazionale dalla formazione del governo Mussolini alla Grande Depressione (1922–1929)*, 2 vols., Rome: Edizioni di Storia e letteratura; Ministero degli Affari Esteri. 2013; *Il trattato di Maastricht e l'unione economica e monetaria*, in *Giulio Andreotti e l'Europa*, edited by Francesco Lefebvre D'Ovidio and Luca Micheletta, Rome: Edizioni di Storia e Letteratura, 2017; *I documenti diplomatici italiani*, Series III, vol. IX (with P. Pastorelli), Rome: Istituto Poligrafico dello Stato; Ministero degli Affari Esteri, 2014; *I documenti diplomatici italiani*, Series III, vol. X (ed.), Rome: Istituto Poligrafico dello Stato; Ministero degli Affari Esteri, 2016; *I documenti diplomatici italiani*, Serie XI, vol. VI (ed.), Rome: Istituto Poligrafico dello Stato; Ministero degli Affari Esteri, 2017; *Documenti sulla politica internazionale dell'Italia, Serie A—Europa Occidentale e Unione Europea, Il "rilancio dell'Europa" dalla Conferenza di Messina ai Trattati di Roma (2 aprile 1955–25 marzo 1957)*, edited by A. Varsori and F. Lefebvre D'Ovidio, Rome: Istituto Poligrafico e Zecca dello Stato, 2018; *Documenti sulla politica internazionale dell'Italia, Serie B—Europa Centrale, Orientale e Russia, La questione dell'Alto Adige/Südtirol: Lo sviluppo della controversia 1964–1969, tomo I (10 dicembre 1964–3 ottobre 1967) e Tomo II (5 ottobre 1967–30 novembre*

1969), edited by Francesco Lefebvre D'Ovidio and Antonio Varsori, Rome: Istituto Poligrafico e Zecca dello Stato, 2019.

Patrick Minford is a British macroeconomist who is Professor of Applied Economics at Cardiff Business School, Cardiff University, a position he has held since 1997.

Minford holds an MSc and PhD from the London School of Economics. He worked at the Ministry of Overseas Development and then as an economic adviser to the Ministry of Finance of Malawi. He then took a position as an economic adviser to Her Majesty's Treasury's External Division. He was appointed as Economics fellow at Manchester University in 1974, becoming editor of the Quarterly Review at the National Institute of Economic and Social Research in 1975, where he began to build the so-called Liverpool Model with Kent Matthews. From 1976 to 1997 he was Edward Gonner Professor of Applied Economics at the University of Liverpool.

He was a Member of Monopolies and Mergers Commission 1990–1996, a Member of H.M. Treasury Panel of Independent Economic Forecasters (originally the "6 Wise Men") from January 1993 to end-1996. He is also a longtime Member of the Academic Council of Economic Affairs, and of the Academic Advisory Board and the Board of Trustees at the Institute of Economic Affairs, and he has been Member of the Editorial Board of several specialized journals. He founded and directs the Liverpool Research Group in Macroeconomics and is Chairman of Economists for Free Trade.

Minford was appointed Commander of the Order of the British Empire in the 1996 New Year Honours for services to economics.

Alberto Mingardi is Associate Professor of History of Political Thought at IULM University in Milan. He holds a PhD in Political Science from University of Pavia. He has published monographs on Herbert Spencer (2011) and Thomas Hodgskin (2016 and 2020). He translated into English, *Antonio Rosmini, The Constitution Under Social Justice* (Lanham, MD: Lexington Books 2003). He edited critical editions of works by Thomas Hodgskin (*Crimine e potere,* Macerata: Liberlibri 2014), Herbert Spencer (*L'uomo contro lo Stato,* Macerata: Liberlibri 2016) and Vilfredo Pareto (*L'ignoranza e il malgoverno,* Macerata: Liberlibri 2018). He is Presidential Scholar in Political Theory at Chapman University in Orange, California. He writes frequently for the popular press. He is one of the founders of the Bruno Leoni Institute in Milan and an adjunct scholar of the Cato Institute in Washington, DC.

Richard Portes is Professor of Economics at London Business School, is Founder and Honorary President of the Centre for Economic Policy Research (CEPR), inaugural holder of the Tommaso Padoa-Schioppa Chair at the European University Institute, and Co-Founder and Co-Chair (1984–2016) of the Board of Economic Policy. He is an elected Fellow of the Econometric Society and of the British Academy. He is Chair of the Advisory Scientific Committee to the European Systemic Risk Board (and Co-Chair of the ESRB's Joint Expert Group on Shadow Banking), of the Steering Committee of the Euro 50 Group, and of the Bellagio Group on the International Economy.

Professor Portes was a Rhodes Scholar and a Fellow of Balliol College, Oxford (of which he is now an Honorary Fellow), and has also taught at Princeton and Birkbeck College (University of London). He has been Distinguished Global Visiting Professor at the Haas Business School, University of California, Berkeley, and Joel Stern Visiting Professor of International Finance at Columbia Business School. He holds three honorary doctorates. He also served as Directeur d'Etudes at the Ecole des Hautes Etudes en Sciences Sociales in Paris (1978–2011).

His current research interests include international macroeconomics, international finance, macroprudential regulation, European bond markets, and European integration. He has written extensively on globalization, sovereign borrowing and debt, European monetary issues, European financial markets, credit default swaps, and international capital flows. Professor Portes was decorated CBE in the 2003 New Year's Honours.

Professor Portes is one of the Academic Directors of the AQR Asset Management Institute at LBS.

Dalibor Rohac is a resident scholar at the American Enterprise Institute (AEI), where he studies European political and economic trends, specifically Central and Eastern Europe, the European Union (EU) and the eurozone, US-EU relations, and the post-communist transitions and backsliding of countries in the former Soviet bloc. He is concurrently a research associate at the Wilfried Martens Centre for European Studies in Brussels and a fellow at Anglo-American University in Prague.

Before joining AEI, Dr. Rohac was affiliated with the Cato Institute's Center for Global Liberty and Prosperity, the Max Beloff Centre at the University of Buckingham, the London-based Legatum Institute, and the Center for the New Europe in Brussels.

Dr. Rohac is the author of *In Defense of Globalism* (Rowman and Littlefield, 2019). His previous book, *Towards an Imperfect Union: A Conservative Case for the EU* (Rowman and Littlefield, 2016), was included on Foreign Affairs magazine's list of best books of 2016. Dr. Rohac has testified before the House Foreign Affairs Committee and has briefed the US Helsinki Commission. His commentary has been published widely in the popular media, including in the Financial Times, Foreign Affairs, Los Angeles Times, The New York Times, The Wall Street Journal, and The Washington Post. His scholarly articles have been featured in policy journals, including Constitutional Political Economy, Journal of Institutional Economics, Kyklos, and Public Choice.

He holds a PhD in Political Economy from King's College London; an MPhil in economics from St Antony's College, University of Oxford; an MA in economics from George Mason University; and a BA in economics from Charles University in Prague.

John B. Taylor is the George P. Shultz Senior Fellow in Economics at the Hoover Institution and the Mary and Robert Raymond Professor of Economics at Stanford University. He chairs the Hoover Institution Working Group on Economic Policy.

An award-winning teacher and researcher specializing in macroeconomics, international economics, and monetary policy, he has served as a senior economist (1976–1977) and member (1989–1991) of the President's Council of Economic Advisers, as Under Secretary of the Treasury for International Affairs (2001–2005), and as a member of the California Governor's Council of Economic Advisors from 1996–1998 and 2005–2010.

Taylor's book *Getting Off Track: How Government Actions and Interventions Caused, Prolonged, and Worsened the Financial Crisis* was one of the first on the 2008 financial crisis; he has since followed up writing or co-editing 15 additional books on restoring economic growth and preventing future crises, including *First Principles: Five Keys to Restoring America's Prosperity* for which he received the Hayek prize.

Before joining the Stanford faculty in 1984, Taylor held positions as Professor of Economics at Princeton University and Columbia University.

List of Figures

List of Tables

CHAPTER 1

Introduction

Francesco Giavazzi, Francesco Lefebvre D'Ovidio, and Alberto Mingardi

A few years ago, a classical liberal philosopher proposed to look at Europe's political history as a conflict between a "Smithian" and a "Colbertist" persuasion. According to Jasay, the first could be labeled "The Feasible is Free" and the latter could be labeled "Permissions Authorize Acts" (Jasay 2002). One has a bottom-up attitude, which tends to consider the working of institutions as bound to fail if they systematically opposed individuals' actions and wills. The other has a top-down attitude and boldly attempts to design better institutions to improve human societies. The latter indulges in the illusion that "the different members of a great

F. Giavazzi
IGIER, Bocconi University, Milan, Italy
e-mail: francesco.giavazzi@unibocconi.it

F. Lefebvre D'Ovidio
Sapienza University of Rome, Rome, Italy
e-mail: francesco.lefebvredovidio@uniroma1.it

A. Mingardi (✉)
IULM University, Milan, Italy

Bruno Leoni Institute, Milan, Italy
e-mail: alberto.mingardi@brunoleoni.org

F. Giavazzi et al. (eds.), *The Liberal Heart of Europe*,
https://doi.org/10.1007/978-3-030-60368-7_1

society" can be arranged "with as much ease as the hand arranges the different pieces upon a chess-board." The first insists that

> the pieces upon the chess-board have no other principle of motion besides that which the hand impresses upon them; but that, in the great chess-board of human society, every single piece has a principle of motion of its own, altogether different from that which the legislature might chuse to impress upon it. If those two principles coincide and act in the same direction, the game of human society will go on easily and harmoniously, and is very likely to be happy and successful. If they are opposite or different, the game will go on miserably, and the society must be at all times in the highest degree of disorder. (Smith [1759] 1982, VI.II.42)

In essence, such conflict has been a constant, subterranean motif in the making of the European Union (EU) as we know it. There was always "a clash of different views of government, between a dirigiste attitude (that is, heavy government intervention in market activities as regulator and coordinator) more common in southern Europe and parts of continental Europe and an Anglo-American attitude, more laissez-faire, which views free markets as well-functioning without much need for centralized policy intervention" (Alesina and Perotti 2004, p. 28).

In the first sixty years of its life (if we begin to count from the establishment of the European Economic Community in 1958), the European Union has been seen by many as mainly a political, dirigiste project and by others as mainly an economic, free trade-leaning one. It has been praised by some and hated by others, exactly for being one or the other.

Politics is always more complex than the words used in politics suggest. These two attitudes coexisted and shaped, and perhaps are still shaping, the development of European integration. Theirs is by no means the only conflict of visions which is affecting the building of Europe: consider the tension between intergovernmentalism (that sees the European institutions as agents of national governments) and functionalism (that sees the process of unification as led by elites transcending national boundaries).

On the one hand, the European project has been envisioned and interpreted as an experiment in economic integration, or perhaps better to say integration-through-the-economy. But there is hardly a blueprint to pursue such a goal.

The very idiom "economic integration" is relatively new in the history of economic thought. Machlup (1977, pp. 4–5) traced it back to a Swedish economist, Eli F. Heckscher, and particularly to its study of Mercantilism, published in Swedish in 1931 but soon translated into English in 1935. In the English translation, the term "disintegration" was used, to refer to "economic disintegration" created by the feudal system, with river tolls and road tolls which impeded trade. The word was soon picked up, "not only for national but also, or chiefly, for international trade" between 1938 and 1942 by economists "Wilhelm Röpke, Ludwig von Mises, Moritz Bonn, Friedrich Hayek, and Folke Hilgerdt." "In December 1942 two papers using our term were presented at the Washington meeting of the American Economic Association, one by Folke Hilgerdt on 'The Case for Multilateral Trade', the other by Antonin Basch on 'Europan Economic Regionalism'" (Machlup 1977, p. 9). Soon enough, in a period of "only a little more than thirty years many proposals for regional and worldwide integration were debated by economists and several of the proposals were actually put into effect. The European Common Market, at first promoted most strongly by economic advisers to the Government of the United States, became a reality, though with serious exceptions" (Machlup 1977, p. 148).

On the other hand, since its beginning, the European project had a clear political aim. It emerged after WWII and because of WWII, in an attempt to offer a solution to the "German problem." The memory of the ghastly aftermath of WWI certainly affected all the European leaders, and so did the international scenario, with the world divided "between the capitalist West and the socialist East" with Germany being "like the dividing door that separated two worlds" (de Souza Silva 2009, p. 5). In the circumstances, Jean Monnet and others started a sort of bricolage unification of Europe, focusing on partial integration in a number of clearly bounded areas (e.g. coal and steel), in order to pursue all the possible steps forward. A unified Europe was always speculated about, since the Ventotene Manifesto (1941), and many argued that "economic" integration was functional to such goals. Yet per se there was and there is "no guarantee that regional integration in economic areas, such as a common market, should lead to political unification down the road" (Spolaore 2013, p. 138).

In the era of Bretton Woods, even before the idea of a common currency came to surface, the ambition of achieving some level of coordination in managing national money supplies gained traction. The financial havoc of the 1930s suggested to many that if the gold standard had failed, so did flexible exchange rates. In a highly influential work, Ragnar Nurkse maintained that "If there is anything that interwar experience has clearly demonstrated, it is that paper currency exchanges cannot be left free to fluctuate from day to day under the influence of market supply and demand" (Nurkse 1944, p. 137). Some sort of currency coordination came thus to be seen as a political goal, as it was needed to avoid the sort of economic disruption which paved the way for authoritarianism in the first half of the century. Nurkse's book was very influential in the early postwar debate on the construction of a European union eventually accompanied by a single European currency.

In solving the "German problem," the European Union was certainly successful, as it became a "tamed power," whose political leaders "exercise power only in multilateral, institutionally mediated systems—in Germany, the EU, the Atlantic Community, and broader international fora—that soften sovereign power" (Katzenstein 1997, p. 2).

The evolution of the European Union is hardly set, as we write. The conflict between the "Smithian" and the "Colbertist" attitudes continue and it is unlikely to be solved by any sort of conclusive settlement.

In his chapter, John Gillingham rightly reminds us that "the founders of the two institutions that eventuated in the EU—the European Coal and Steel Community (ECSC) of 1952 and the European Economic Community (EEC) of 1958 were senior civil servants and diplomats rather than intellectuals or economists—and the motivation behind their work had less to do with any particular theory than with shared experience, above all that of the still recent world war" (infra, Chap. 7).

Yet this book has been put together under the assumption that there is such thing as a "Liberal Heart of Europe." A number of scholars are convinced that "Europe can and should provide the oversight and control over capitalism that the nation-state once did" (Berman 2006, p. 214). The future of the EU seems to be distinctively linked to this challenge. In her famous—or infamous—Bruges speech, Margaret Thatcher outlined her own agenda for Europe, which she saw as alternative to the extant consensus. She called for "action to free markets, action to widen choice, action to reduce government intervention" and "continue the process of removing barriers to trade" (Thatcher 1988). Thatcher was aligned with an older tradition of criticism of the EU, of the Smithian bent, that always tended to stress that while "the removal of obstacles to inter-member trade is per se clearly an immense stride toward freedom of trade," yet "in combination with the ring-fence tariff, freedom of inter-member trade is a system of discrimination" (Shenfield [1963] 2016). In more recent years, using a rather infelicitous metaphor many spoke of a "Fortress Europe," which could gain power in a globalized world, through its common system of tariffs and a common management of immigration.

These criticisms may tend to obscure the strong "Smithian" element, in the very making of what later turned to be the European Union. Such an element was profoundly appreciated by our late friend Alberto Giovannini. Alberto, an outstanding macroeconomist but also a man of the world, was profoundly involved in easing obstacles to cross-border payments in Europe. He was the chairman of what later came to be known as the Giovannini Group on Cross-border Clearing and Settlement Arrangements in the EU, launched by the European Commission in 1996. He was also a member of the Advisory Scientific Committee of the European Systemic Risk Board, from its inception in 2011.

It is telling that, in 2018, Alberto felt the need to convene a conference on the influence of Anglo-Saxon liberal thinking in the early years of the European project. The eurozone crisis has already contributed to changing the institutional infrastructure of the EU—as the COVID-19 pandemic will do, even more profoundly, some years later. Alberto wanted to revisit "the liberal heart of Europe," focus its implications, and revive the spirits of the key figures who imagined it well ahead of the time. We were privileged to be his partners in such an effort, organizing—under the auspices of Istituto Bruno Leoni and in collaboration with the Centro Studi sul Federalismo—in Turin 2019 a conference that Alberto, by then severely ill, could not attend.

We maintain that the conference essays collected in this book, or at least some of them, document that Anglo-Saxon (Smithian) influence has been powerful, although its role had been forgotten in the studies that reconstruct the genesis of the European project in the postwar. Alberto's intuition was right. Digging into the history of ideas was one of Alberto's many gifts and this book is one such example. His passion and open-mindedness in so doing are well testified by the contributors to this book, a fair number of whom were his personal friends.

The book is not, and could not be, exclusively backward-looking. European institutions are hardly a "given": they are still unfolding, developing, changing. We hope this book will shed light on the past, but also provide with some glimpse of what the future may be like.

Michael Burda sees "European integration" as "a process measured in centuries and millennia rather than decades." Building on the insights of Herbert Giersch, Burda considers the German approach to the European

Union as an offspring of "German geography and history, as well as sociology." He considers that the EU has been a failure in making the average citizen understand the benefits of economic integration, as it is proven by "its parlous image in the eyes of its own citizens, even in countries that have benefited the most from membership *on average*."

In his contribution, Richard Portes weighs on how different the so-called postwar consensus presented clear-cut national nuances. Portes begins with examining the Italian version of the so-called European federalism, focusing on the "Manifesto di Ventotene" and linking it with "liberal socialism, or social liberalism," a short-lived but highly influential intellectual movement whose key champions (including Ernesto Rossi, one of the authors of the "Manifesto di Ventotene") were "convinced of the complementarity of domestic liberal socialism and European federalism." Portes underlines the role played by the United States, in the context of the then beginning Cold War, in the promotion of intra-European economic cooperation.

Critics of the EU—or, more generally, those who made a sport of calling on "austerity measures"—like to denounce Ordoliberalism (*Ordnungspolitik*), as the main set of ideas which allegedly shaped the European Union. This does hardly fit the narrative of the Bruges speech or more generally the current predominant English attitude toward the European Union. Stefan Kolev provides a comprehensive outlook of how Ordoliberals like Wilhelm Röpke, Ludwig Erhard, and Alfred Müller-Armack considered the early beginnings of European integration. Even back then, they considered the possible evolution of the European project as something that could either yield a "'large Switzerland', i.e. a politically decentralized entity which is economically integrated internally as well as non-protectionist externally, or a 'large France', i.e. a politically centralized entity which is economically integrated internally but protectionist externally." Smith versus Colbert again. The Ordoliberal vision of the future of European integration was hardly univocal, in spite of over-simplification that are increasingly common these days.

Rohac and Mingardi focus instead on three other classical liberal thinkers: Luigi Einaudi, Ludwig von Mises, and F.A. Hayek. Einaudi was a father of the European project; Mises and Hayek are seldom recognized as such. They focus in particular on Hayek's 1939 "The Economic Conditions of Interstate Federalism," which envisioned something vaguely similar to the future EU, stressing that both Hayek and Einaudi took it "as a given that a federation would have to use a common monetary unit." The opposition to monetary nationalism was one of the classical liberal arguments in favor of supranational bodies: these arguments (dear to Einaudi since the 1910s) became stronger as Europe was wrecked by the clash of nationalisms. Rohac and Mingardi stress that "although the efforts of modern classical liberals revolve primarily around an intellectual agenda for the domestic reform of institutions and policies leading to a reduction in the size, scope and discretionary powers of the state, it is impossible to dissociate them from questions of the international economic order." Still, one may argue that classical liberalism in international affairs was even less successful than in internal affairs.

In his chapter John Gillingham, a prominent and controversial scholar of the European process, provides a thorough outline of the thought of Jean Monnet. Gillingham moves us away from history of economic and political thought. His key point is that "often described as a work in progress, and thus immune to definitive judgment, a meaningful description of the Brussels governance structure continues to elude scholars." The EU "is neither a genuine nation-state nor a true international organization but merely a hybrid trans-national institution resting on murky legal foundations and with an ill-defined operational sphere." In his contribution, Gillingham cites again Ludwig Erhard, who would have preferred a free trade area, which would have "merely eliminated tariff barriers between member states," but whose views were overridden by German chancellor Konrad Adenauer, who preferred to go for the EEC, that "was designed as a customs union with a common external tariff." Once again, German positions on the European project look more nuanced than what critics believe.

In the subsequent sections of the book, the authors approach other key episodes. The 1980s is investigated in the essays by Jacques de Larosière, Patrick Minford, and Otmar Issing.

De Larosière considers the changes in the European institutions in the 1980s as basically the outcome of the end of the Cold War, of which German unification was a consequence (Issing writes in more detail on this), and of the global push towards "deregulation" and "privatization." He points out that "for the Community as a whole, the move towards deregulation accelerated the 'internationalization' of European markets and their integration into the 'Atlantic' world ... deregulation—which was not in the main EEC tradition—became a factor of European integration."

This may suggest that the role of Margaret Thatcher, in future histories of the EU, may not be remembered as an enemy's, but rather one of an accelerator of the European project. While Thatcher, particularly in later years, proposed a form of disengagement from the European project, it was Alberto Giovannini's conviction that her reforms and her political rhetoric strengthened the unifying tendencies. It is certainly hard to imagine the European Central Bank (ECB) without Thatcher embracing "monetarism" as her banner (and indeed at the time both her Chancellors of the Exchequer, Geoffrey Howe and Nigel Lawson, favored some sort of monetary unification and the European Exchange Rate Mechanism). De Larosière himself points out that "the independence of Central Banks—as well as monetarism—became a common objective" because of the change of attitude in the government/market balance which was in part the result of Thatcherism and its success.

Minford provides a neat précis of Margaret Thatcher's economic reforms. Minford reasons on how Thatcher's reforms "came to be politically possible, given the large-scale forces arrayed against them," and finds a key supporter in the "skilled working class" and reminds us that "the defeat of inflation was extremely popular: inflation, with its effects in redistributing resources to those lucky or smart enough to do well from inflation, had become highly unpopular."

Another "German perspective" on the road to the EU is provided by Issing, in an important chapter that benefits from his own reminiscences, at a key turn of European integration. "Germany's reunification," Issing reminds us, "had turned almost all economic relations upside down," determining circumstances that the Bundesbank had to face with its "pragmatic monetarism" (a coinage of Issing's). Issing testifies that "the decision to move towards European monetary union was taken before the fall of the Wall. Ultimately, German reunification added momentum to a journey that had already begun." The decision to go for a monetary union is connected to the fact that "for France it was hard, and in the longer run unacceptable, to have its monetary policy 'made in Frankfurt'" and thus "since all attempts to share the responsibility for monetary policy with existing national currencies had failed, France finally accepted the idea of a European central bank and a common currency."

The later section of the book deals with our current predicament.

John Taylor provides us some "perspective on the euro." Taylor ranks the ECB favorably in transparency and communication and as "voice for structural and market-based reforms in individual countries." Yet he points to the Bank's "deviations from rules or strategies" which "have resulted in a move toward a more interventionist, less market-based institution" in recent years. A leading voice for monetary rules versus discretion, Taylor sees the ECB as moving away from such principles, with "an increased use of discretionary interventions." Recent years have certainly seen central banks evolving in largely unpredictable ways—and certainly we have not seen the end of such evolution yet.

Bénassy-Quéré and Giavazzi also focus on European institutions from a financial standpoint, attempting to consider how we may deal with long-lasting effects of the COVID-19 pandemic, a shock which has accelerated the European project to an extent inconceivable before the event, but has left a legacy of debt. Bénassy-Quéré and Giavazzi discuss the optimal way to deal with it. They suggest that its cost should be spread onto future generations, in a similar way as after a war.

In his chapter, Leszek Balcerowicz examines the backlash against globalization. Balcerowicz distinguishes between a "crude anti-globalism" and a more intellectually ambitious version of the same set of ideas that he criticizes in detail. In one way or another, a dominant feature of the European debate, all over the continent, has been the resurgence of nationalism in recent times. Nationalists have often been the better communicators, in different countries. Balcerowicz remarks that "globalization is too often blamed for the results of bad policies, especially those which hamper individuals' adjustment to new pressures, and those which encourage them to take excessive risks." Yet clear analytical distinctions between causes and effects often escape the wider audience.

Edmond Alphandéry, in his contribution, deals precisely with the nationalist political narratives, which are often centered, in recent years, on the allegedly poor performance of the eurozone in the financial crisis. The shock "worked as a lever for Europe to move forward and progress," but when specific policies were no longer merely discussed among technocrats and experts, but entered the public debate at large, they were typically misrepresented, fueling populists. "In order to restore confidence, member states have to put their houses in order." But it would be wrong to consider this a process whose costs are not matched by benefits "confidence based on sound economic policies is a key factor for the return to prosperity and social progress."

As the reader may see, this is a pluralist book, which was put together because of a thirst for genuine and open-minded reflections, not having some definitive answers in mind.

The questions were largely the product of Alberto Giovannini's curiosity. They were reflected in the program of the conference whose proceedings we have collected here.

For that conference Alberto set a very high bar.

He explained the aim of the conference in a document "Some Introductory Thoughts" that is reproduced next and assigned to the authors he had invited seven questions. Going through the list the reader will realize that more than a list of questions to inform a conference, this is a wide research agenda spanning politics and economics. It will come as no surprise that the conference proceedings collected in this volume come short of addressing, let aside answering, these questions.

The conference, as all conferences, soon took on a life of its own. But the legacy of Alberto's introductory thoughts extends beyond this conference and this volume, which we hope will honor his tremendous intellectual curiosity and his fecund contributions.

The questions the chapters in this book aim to answer, far more than the way they answer them, can be seen as the starting point of an investigation which should be central to the concerns of European economists and political scientists alike. This research agenda is Alberto's gift and his legacy.

References

Alesina, Alberto, and Roberto Perotti. 2004. The European Union: A Politically Incorrect View. *Journal of Economic Perspectives* 18: 27–48.

Berman, Sheri. 2006. *The Primacy of Politics. Social Democracy and the Making of Europe's Twentieth Century.* Cambridge: Cambridge University Press.

De Souza Silva, Karine. 2009. Pedagogy of Peace: The Contribution of Jean Monnet to the Construction of the European Union. *Jean Monnet/Robert Schuman Paper Series* 9: 5. Miami, FL: University of Miami and Florida European Union Center of Excellence at Florida International University (FIU). http://aei.pitt.edu/11046/1/Silva-MonnetLong09edi.pdf. Accessed 20 July 2020.

Jasay, Anthony de. 2002. Between Colbert and Adam Smith. *Cato Journal* 21: 359–367.

Katzenstein, Peter, ed. 1997. United Germany in an Integrating Europe. In *Tamed Power: Germany in Europe.* Ithaca, NY: Cornell University Press.

Machlup, Fritz. 1977. *A History of Thought of Economic Integration.* London: Macmillan.

Nurkse, Ragnar. 1944. *The International Currency Experience.* Geneva: League of Nations.

Shenfield, Arthur A. [1963] 2016. *The Two Faces of the Common Market*. Chicago Booth Review Winter 2016/17. Chicago: University of Chicago Booth School of Business. https://review.chicagobooth.edu/economics/archive/two-faces-common-market. Accessed 20 July 2020.

Smith, Adam. [1759] 1982. *The Theory of Moral Sentiments*, ed. D.D. Raphael and A.L. Macfie. Indianapolis: Liberty Fund.

Spolaore, Enrico. 2013. What Is European Integration Really About? A Political Guide for Economists. *Journal of Economic Perspectives* 27: 125–144.

Thatcher, Margaret. 1988. *Speech to the College of Europe*. Speech delivered at the Belfry of Bruges, Belgium, September 20. https://www.margaretthatcher.org/document/107332. Accessed 20 July 2020.

CHAPTER 2

Some Introductory Thoughts

Alberto Giovannini

Keynes was right when he wrote that economists have gained a very large status in our societies: "The ideas of economists and political philosophers, both when they are right and when they are wrong, are more powerful than is commonly understood. Indeed, the world is ruled by little else. [...] Soon or late, it is ideas, not vested interests, which are dangerous for good or evil" (Keynes 1936, p. 383). Yes, ideas can be dangerous. But the dynamics of economic policymaking cannot be reduced to the shallow connection of political actions to past, and possibly outmoded, economists.

There is much more than hinted at by Keynes. With the benefit of hindsight, it is important to try and identify which ideas were right and which weren't. And this leads us to an even deeper question: how much of a firm base is economic knowledge to those in charge of policy decisions?

As we recall the evolution of economic policymaking starting from the nineteenth century, we recognize conscious decisions of

A. Giovannini (Deceased) (✉)

F. Giavazzi et al. (eds.), *The Liberal Heart of Europe*,
https://doi.org/10.1007/978-3-030-60368-7_2

policymakers which now appear based on faulty reasoning, leading to momentous consequences which lasted for many decades. We find public debates dominated by economic concepts for which there is no precise or generally agreed meaning, decisions based on illusions. And when, in some cases, the circle is closed, we find that economic reality returns to politics with a vengeance. But in these cases, politicians often do not see the lesson and, tragically, convince themselves of completely different lessons.

For all these reasons, the meeting of politics and economics is a phenomenon of epic proportions, resembling a struggle: an epic struggle. Our objective in this conference will be to understand this struggle exploring one of the most important phenomena of recent history: the process of European integration. We chose it for two main reasons: first, we have been close observers of this process in recent years; second, we find in this process many clues that may help us dispel the fog of this struggle.

Here is a list of problems, attempting to find answers.

- The sequencing of reforms: why it seems that economic reforms take precedence over political reforms? In other words, why economic institutions appear to change before political institutions?

It would seem more logical to start from political reforms creating institutions that would then support the opening and integration of markets. One would start from the civil code, from harmonized taxation, from the coordination of fiscal policies. This would in turn open the way to free circulation of goods.

This however is not the sequence that appears to be more frequent. Germany, for example, started from harmonizing customs, railways, and currency while maintaining some 300 independent and sovereign political units. Later came political integration, after economic integration, and had been achieved. And it was overall a success story. The European integration process also started with economic reforms and is proceeding with ups and downs. The Italian unification experience, on the other hand, followed the opposite sequence, and it was not an obvious success.

Thinking about sequencing we need to try and answer two questions: (1) What explains the sequencing we observe? (2) What are the consequences of this apparently lopsided way to proceed?

- The European project occurs at the end of a century that has seen an unprecedented growth in the role of government in societies: is this the product of a sequence of accidents that occurred in the twentieth century or a natural evolution of modern market-based economies? How has the debate on European integration addressed the problem of the size of government?

The broad historical facts are, on the front of political ideas, that at the beginning of the twentieth century in market economies political movements developed calling for the state to ensure a minimum level of welfare for its citizens. Thereafter two world wars brought about a quantum leap in the size of the government in the US and Great Britain, which did not return to pre-war levels after the conflicts were over. Economists use a rule to define the role of governments: whenever markets fail there is in principle a reason for the government to step in. This is a rather strict criterion: for example, going back to Samuelson's "chocolate" paper, why should the government save for the retirement of its citizens? However, there should be a mirror criterion to find the proper equilibrium: the size of the government should be limited by government failures. Here one should cite the Lange-Lerner and other debates on the failure of command economies due to the impossible complexities of managing them, but also the numerous cases reported by Hernando de Soto on the ineffectiveness of government and the problem of entrenched interests and corruption. Across European states, there is a variety of views and experiences on the role of government, not a single view. Is such a variety of views reflected in the European treaties? And is the intergovernmental character of the treaties an obstacle to a strategy aimed at finding the proper size of government in Europe?

- How did monetary union occur? Was there an active role by interest groups directly affected by this reform? Or was it a movement driven by élites?

Contrary to the mainstream in political science, it is hard to find any connection between the progress of monetary union and the economic interests in monetary union of different groups in the participating countries. This is in large part because the economic impact of the elimination of a country's currency is not a topic with which politicians, let alone public opinion, are familiar. Perceptions on national currencies are linked with perceptions of independence (or sovereignty), in rather abstract terms (the currency a symbol of the nation, like the flag). This is a topic that allows us to illustrate one of the phenomena discussed in the introduction. Decision-makers based their actions on illusions. When reality came back to haunt them, they still interpret events in the wrong way.

– What is the role of monetary policy in a region like the euro area? Does the optimum currency area argument hold? How should the central bank balance the objective of inflation with that of financial stability?

That brings us to the role of monetary policy. The public debate is full of slogans about some presumed macroeconomic role for monetary policy, influencing economic activity and dealing with economic imbalances. This clashes with what is known in monetary economics. The financial crisis has brought to the center another problem: central banks were born to deal with financial crises, but the treaty has not really equipped the European Central Bank (ECB) for that task. The ECB however seems to have found a basis to act also in the realm of financial stability, and banking supervision, which was very prominently absent from the charter of the central bank.

– What is fiscal policy?

The term is used with the same ease as monetary policy, but it is much less grounded on systematic analysis. It is not at all clear whether one can call some government action fiscal policy and whether the fiscal surplus or deficit has a reliable impact on the economy. We side with Eric Leeper in thinking that as long as it keeps practicing alchemy, fiscal policy will be too political and too confused to help. Fiscal policy is inherited from modifications of the Keynesian model and has been given a key role in policy decisions by the US Employment Act of 1946. Our working assumption is that since all of fiscal policy is redistributive (from taxpayers to recipients of government spending, from current generations to future generations, or vice versa), understanding its impact on the economy is a rather difficult affair. This difficulty is usually brushed aside by politicians whose access to the levers of government spending and taxation can give them large consensus with their constituencies and, in the worst cases, easy ways to enrich themselves. In Europe, fiscal policy is considered mainly as the management of the government budget balance. The concern of European treaties is that budget imbalances should not generate instabilities in the

Union. The simple rules that are part of the treaties are based on the theory that the political process is inherently biased toward excessive deficits and, as such, it needs a counterbalance. We want to determine whether the governance of the European Union has seen some type of evolution on the issue of fiscal policy and what could be future avenues.

- Related to the above, what is the debate in Europe of so-called austerity versus expansionary policies?

The debate on austerity versus expansionary policies has been present in Europe at least since the setup of the European Monetary System (EMS) and, in international fora like the Organisation for Economic Co-operation and Development, it has been the central issue to be brought up in policy bodies such as the Working Party 3 (WP3). This debate is in our view used by politicians for objectives that do not tightly coincide with the overall well-being of their countries. We intend to expose these distortions and explore whether there may be a more reliable way to discuss coordination among European governments.

- The problem of the moving bar: Every economic reform in Europe aimed at integrating markets raises new problems and makes new barriers emerge, which call for further, and deeper, programs for reforms. What are the implications of this? Is there a natural stopping point?

The two examples we want to illustrate are the monetary union and capital markets liberalization. It has been found that monetary union was insufficient because most money is commercial bank money, and therefore banking union was needed to make monetary union work. But banking union raised a whole list of difficult reforms including the management of deposit insurance, the management of banking supervision, and the management of banks' resolutions. Similarly, the liberalization of capital movements was seen, erroneously, as a sufficient condition to ensure capital markets integration. Then came the Financial Services Action Plan (FSAP) a long list of directives aimed at integrating capital markets. Then the movement to integrate financial markets infrastructure (in which, among other things, it was suggested that civil codes needed amendments because the concept of ownership of securities was different from country to country). But that was not enough: now there is the plan for Capital Markets Union (CMU). And there are already observers who point to the need of uniform bankruptcy codes, for example. It seems to us that these reforms create a momentum that is exclusively originating from the logic of making things work well. But where does this lead?

Many of the issues listed above are amenable to economic analysis, which we will definitely apply. However, these are not essays in economics, nor are they essays in politics *stricto sensu*. Our aim should be to understand an important historical process through a special lens: that of the interaction of politics and economics. Hence our method should wed economic analysis with the analysis of political actors and events.

Alberto Giovannini 1955–2019

2.1 Alberto Giovannini (1955–2019): Selected Scientific Contributions

Clerc, Laurent, Alberto Giovannini, Sam Langfield, Tuomas Peltonen, Richard Portes, and Martin Scheicher. 2016. *Indirect Contagion: The Policy Problem*. ESRB Occasional Paper 9, January. Frankfurt am Main: European Systemic Risk Board.

Giovannini, Alberto. 2013. *Risk-Free Assets in Financial Markets*. BIS Papers 72. Basel: Bank for International Settlements.

Giavazzi, Francesco, and Alberto Giovannini. 2011. Central Banks and the Financial System. In *Handbook of Central Banking, Financial Regulation and Supervision After the Financial Crisis*, ed. S. Eijffinger and D. Masciandaro, 3–29. Cheltenham: Edward Elgar.

Giovannini, Alberto. 2010. Why the European Securities Market Is Not Fully Integrated. In *Europe and the Euro*, ed. Alberto Alesina and Francesco Giavazzi, 255–283. Chicago: University of Chicago Press

The Giovannini Group. 2002. *Cross-Border Clearing and Settlement Arrangements in the European Union. Brussels, November 2001*. Economic Papers of the European Commission, Directorate-General for Economic and Financial Affairs 163. Brussels: European Communities.

The Giovannini Group. 2003. *Second Report on EU Clearing and Settlement Arrangements*. Brussels: European Commission.

Chen, Zhaohui, and Alberto Giovannini. 1998. Estimating Expected Exchange Rates Under Target Zones. *International Journal of Theoretical and Applied Finance* 1: 43–59.

Chen, Zhaohui, and Alberto Giovannini. 1997. The Determinants of Realignment Expectations Under the EMS: Some Empirical Regularities. *European Economic Review* 9: 1687–1707.

Giovannini, Alberto. 1996. Introduction. In *The Microstructure of Foreign Exchange Markets*, ed. Jeffrey A. Frankel, Giampaolo Galli and Alberto Giovannini, 1–16. Chicago: University of Chicago Press.

Giovannini, Alberto. 1995. *The Debate on Money in Europe*. Cambridge, MA, London: The MIT Press.

De Gregorio, Jose, Alberto Giovannini, and Holger C. Wolf. 1994. International Evidence on Tradables and Nontradable Inflation. *European Economic Review* 6: 1225.

Giovannini, Alberto, R. Glenn Hubbard, and Joel Slemrod, eds. 1993. *Studies in International Taxation*. Chicago: University of Chicago Press.
Giovannini, Alberto, and Martha de Melo. 1993. Government Revenue from Financial Repression. *American Economic Review* 4: 953–963.
Giovannini, Alberto, and Philippe Jorion. 1993. Time-Series Tests of a Non-Expected-Utility Model of Asset Pricing. *European Economic Review* 5: 1083–1100.
Giovannini, Alberto. 1992. Bretton Woods and Its Precursors: Rules Versus Discretion in the History of International Monetary Regimes. In *Retrospective on the Bretton Woods System: Lessons for International Monetary Reform*, ed. Michael D. Bordo and Barry Eichengreen, 109–154. Chicago: University of Chicago Press.
Giovannini, Alberto, and Jae Won Park. 1992. Capital Controls and International Trade Finance. *Journal of International Economics* 33: 285–304.
Giovannini, Alberto. 1992. Target Zones and the Distribution of Exchange Rates: An Estimation Method. *Economics Letters* 40: 83–89.
Giovannini, Alberto. 1992. The Currency Reform as the Last Stage of Economic and Monetary Union: Some Policy Questions. *European Economic Review* 36: 433–444.
Giovannini, Alberto, and James R. Hines. 1991. Capital Flight and Tax Competition: Are There Viable Solutions to Both Problems? In *European Financial Integration*, ed. Alberto Giovannini and Colin Mayer, 172–210. Cambridge, MA: Cambridge University Press.
Giovannini, Alberto. 1991. International Capital Mobility and Tax Avoidance. *Banca Nazionale del Lavoro Quarterly Review* 177: 197–223.
Giovannini, Alberto, and Pamela Labadie. 1991. "Asset Prices and Interest Rates in Cash-In-Advance Models." *Journal of Political Economy* 6: 1215–1251.
Giovannini, Alberto, Richard N. Cooper, and Robert E. Hall. 1990. European Monetary Reform: Progress and Prospects. *Brookings Papers on Economic Activity* 21: 217–292.
Dornbusch, Rudiger, and Alberto Giovannini. 1990. Monetary Policy in the Open Economy. In *Handbook of Monetary Economics*, vol. II, ed. Benjamin Friedman and Frank Hahn, 1231–1303. Amsterdam: North-Holland-Elsevier Science Publishers.
Giavazzi, Francesco, and Alberto Giovannini. 1990. Can the European Monetary System Be Copied Outside Europe? Lessons from Ten Years of Monetary Policy Coordination in Europe. In *International Policy*

Coordination and Exchange Rate Fluctuations, ed. William H. Branson, Jacob A. Frenkel, and Morris Goldstein, 247–278. Chicago: University of Chicago Press.

Giovannini, Alberto, and Marcello De Cecco, eds. 1990. *A European Central Bank: Perspectives on Monetary Unification After Ten Years of the EMS*. Cambridge, NY, Port Chester, Melbourne, and Sydney: Cambridge University Press.

Giavazzi, Francesco, and Alberto Giovannini. 1989. *Limiting Exchange-Rate Flexibility: The European Monetary System*. Cambridge, MA: MIT Press.

Giovannini, Alberto. 1989. How Do Fixed-Exchange-Rates Regimes Work: Evidence from The Gold Standard, Bretton Woods and the EMS. In *Blueprints for Exchange Rate Management*, ed, Marcus Miller, Barry Eichengreen, and Richard Portes, 13–41. New York: Academic Press, Ltd.

Giovannini, Alberto, and Philippe Jorion. 1989. The Time-Variation of Risk and Return in the Foreign Exchange and Stock Markets. *Journal of Finance* XLIV: 307–325.

Giovannini, Alberto. 1989. "Uncertainty and Liquidity." *Journal of Monetary Economics* 23: 239–258.

Giovannini, Alberto, and Julio J. Rotemberg. 1989. Exchange Rate Dynamics with Sticky Prices: The Deutsche Mark, 1974–1982. *Journal of Business and Economic Statistics* 7: 169–178.

Giavazzi, Francesco, and Alberto Giovannini. 1989. "Monetary Policy Interactions under Managed Exchange Rates." *Economica* (New Series) 56: 199–213.

Giavazzi, Francesco, and Alberto Giovannini. 1987. Models of the EMS: Is Europe a Deutsche-Mark Monetary Area? In *Global Macroeconomics: Policy Conflicts and Co-operation*, ed. Ralph C. Bryant and Richard Portes, 237–272. London: Macmillan.

Reference

Keynes, John M. 1936. *General Theory of Employment, Interest and Money*. London: Macmillan.

PART I

The European "Postwar Consensus" and the European Project

CHAPTER 3

The Origins of the Idea of European Integration: A German Perspective

Michael C. Burda

My first encounter with Alberto Giovannini was at a Centre for Economic Policy Research (CEPR) summer meeting in the late 1980s. I remember him as a tall, almost overpowering physical presence, a tough but kind-hearted European, belying all possible stereotypes one might try to attach to him. I have fond memories of exchanges with Alberto at academic conferences, and his papers on exchange rate regimes showed the strong influence of both his MIT training and his dissertation advisor, Rudi Dornbusch. His research reflected a passion for issues of international payments as well as monetary and fiscal policy in the European context, and many of his papers betrayed a suspicion that Germany would play a dominant and possibly decisive role in any future monetary union. I was sad when Alberto moved on from academics to finance and financial policy, but could see that he was destined to leave a mark on the practical world. I am even sadder now that he has left us, much too soon.

M. C. Burda (✉)
Humboldt University of Berlin, Berlin, Germany
e-mail: burda@wiwi.hu-berlin.de

F. Giavazzi et al. (eds.), *The Liberal Heart of Europe*,
https://doi.org/10.1007/978-3-030-60368-7_3

European integration is a process measured in centuries and millennia rather than decades. It is layered with historical, political, and sociological dimensions largely absent from the integration of the US-American states, so comparisons must be appropriately qualified. Europe lacks a common idealism (freedom from tyranny, manifest destiny, the American dream, a "city on a hill") or linguistic dimension (English as opposed to French, German or Spanish). We must admit that European integration is merely accompanied, but hardly determined, by economic logic. Without economics, it is certainly difficult to follow the path of European history; yet without reference to historical, geographic, linguistic, and cultural contexts, it is simply impossible to account for the twists and turns of its economic development.

For more than 20 years, I have given a popular course for bachelor students that applies basic principles of undergraduate macro- and microeconomics to the challenges of European integration. In that course, I adopt Eichengreen's (1990) position that deep integration of regions involves factor markets as much as trade in goods. Yet the peoples of Europe, who lead parallel existences with recourse to their own histories, traditions, languages, and cultures, seem doomed to block Mundell's (1957) substitution theorem of factor mobility for trade, in contrast to the US experience. At the very least, Europe's proclivity to resist transnational migration puts much more burden on capital mobility for solving Europe's integration challenge. Capital mobility, which will ultimately mirror chronic trade imbalances otherwise accepted or ignored within a nation, can become a threat to unity in a loose confederation of states.

In my remarks, I will sketch the role of these aspects in shaping the German view of European economic integration. In doing so, I will stress the role of geography and heterogeneity, especially in the recent century. National features such as historical accidents, population density, tribalism, climate, and especially centrality have all conditioned European integration and each member's perception of its benefits and costs. Many of these ideas, particularly concerning the role of centrality and location, have been important in guiding German thinking on European integration. This implicates the EU's marketing of the economic integration process and of the "four freedoms." When the conference was held, the discussion centered on Brexit and its consequences for deeper European integration. Brexit has been since overshadowed by the corona pandemic, possibly the greatest threat to European integration since World War II (WWII).

3.1 The Inexorability of European Economic Integration: The Consequence of "Unstoppable" Modern Forces?

If we define economic integration as the pursuit of an efficient allocation made possible by the union of otherwise autarkic regions—possibly with starkly different levels of development at the outset as measured by capital-labor ratios or wealth-GDP ratios—then this process could be achieved in at least four ways:

- Internal capital accumulation à la Solow/Swan (Solow 1956; Swan 1956): home-grown economic growth enabled by common technologies, levels of infrastructure, regulations, and rule of law, leading to unconditional convergence described by Barro and Sala-i-Martin (1991, 1992).
- Trade: the movement of goods and services across national boundaries along the lines of Heckscher-Ohlin trade in products with different factor content (e.g., Feenstra 2003), with regions exporting those goods that utilize the relatively abundant factor more intensively.
- Capital mobility: foreign direct investment across regions, raising capital intensity in capital-poor regions while lowering it in those that are capital-rich.
- Labor mobility: movement of people of working age across regional boundaries, increasing the concentration of labor where it is wanting (Mundell 1957).

My vision of integration makes no appeal to notions of fairness or equity across household or generations, as I have no idea how to think of a fair distribution of resources across Europe's many and diverse peoples. Nor does this concept address policy coordination between nations and regions. In the absence of supply-side convergence—an alignment of institutional and legal frameworks—macroeconomic policy coordination becomes more and more important in response to shocks of both symmetric and asymmetric nature. I will, however, leave this dimension of European integration for others to study.

For centuries, geography and history—natural boundaries, national borders and good old European tribalism—held back the forces of economic integration. They were unleashed after WWII, stimulated by the formation of the European Economic Community, accelerated by the Single European Act 1987, and culminated in the Maastricht Treaty of 1992. They led to increasingly productive value-added chains, the dismantling of inefficient capital controls, and the passporting of most forms of human capital, a new European currency, and to a period of generalized growth and prosperity that arguably put Western Europe within spitting distance of the United States. It all came to a screeching halt after the financial crisis of 2008–09, the European sovereign debt crisis in its wake, and Brexit.

3.2 General Challenges to European Economic Integration

The challenges to European economic integration closely resemble the general obstacles to a welfare-improving monetary union (Mundell 1961, Johnson 1971, Baldwin and Wyplosz 2019). First and foremost, heterogeneity of preferences for efficiency, economic freedom, rule of law—but also for leisure, the environment, and overall quality of life— pose a significant impediment to the regional convergence predictions of the Solow model. Economic geography and history in Europe reinforce this heterogeneity, leading to permanent level differences of total factor productivity and GDP per capita across countries, and inevitably to demands for transfers across national boundaries. The *acquis communautaire* reflects the importance of harmonizing underlying conditions *ex ante* leading to common unconditional convergence of EU regions and nations and maintaining them going forward.

Harmonization of tariff and factor market policies are the central accelerant of the European integration process. Because these policies are inherently national, gains flowing from economic integration are also likely to have a strong *national* component (meaning that some countries will always gain more than others, and some may even be immiserated), possibly leading to demands for redistribution of integration gains across national boundaries. Increasing returns to scale, especially evident in the presence of intra-industry trade, will necessarily lead to an uneven distribution of rewards to those countries with "winner" products. Furthermore, the divergence of winners and losers within countries are likely to be larger when mechanisms for redistribution are largely absent. These pressures intensify if factor price equalization fails, leading to large groups of loser factors ready to move to countries with higher factor returns.

Sadly, when losers from free trade are uncompensated, national interests often can trump liberal, free-market arguments for economic integration. Figure 3.1 displays the result of the recent Eurobarometer survey on globalization—understood as increasing trade integration at both the European and international levels—and reveals surprisingly negative reception in many EU countries. The diversity of perceptions of and preferences for economic integration is just as striking as the asymmetry of shocks or the lack of labor mobility. These preferences are persistent as well: for at least a decade, the Nordics, the Baltics, the "Low Countries," and Germany have consistently seen globalization as a positive force, while closed and larger European countries harbor negative views of integration. Greece and Portugal show that periphery status is neither necessary nor sufficient for "globalization aversion."

Perceived gains and losses from European trade integration are even more asymmetric when national industries and jobs are added to the balance. Losses may be strongly correlated with industries with national identity, and countries are unequipped, unprepared, or unwilling to redistribute gains from trade. Given that asymmetry, what chance does Europe have,

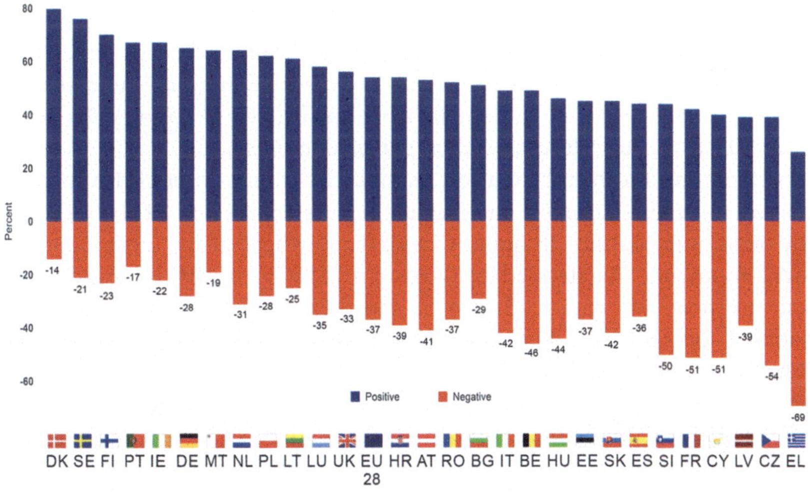

Fig. 3.1 European public opinion on globalization—the response "no opinion" is excluded. (*Source*: Special Eurobarometer 416 [European Commission 2017]). (Color figure online)

given its long history of cultural, ethnic, and religious rivalries, of addressing and accommodating future unevenly distributed gains and losses from economic integration? How can Europe regulate activities with inherent external effects, such as consumer safety, environmental protection, finance, or health? How can this be organized within a liberal economic order without significant losses of national sovereignty, that is, *without* recourse to a supranational state?

3.3 Challenges to Germany Posed by European Integration: History's Doormat or Herbert Giersch's Volcano?

Until now, I have described challenges facing any European country facing the cost-benefit calculation for more and deeper integration; without redistribution, a natural limit exists beyond which incremental losses outweigh potential gains. Germany in particular has profited significantly from the Single Market, the Maastricht Treaty, the Schengen Agreement, and most of all the euro, possibly much more than the average EU member. While the median German voter might see their success as a reflection of hard work, diligence, and *Ordnungspolitik*, a cynic might chalk it up to the "luck of the draw," in which economic geography and history play the decisive role. Just as the corona pandemic randomly picked its initial victims, I am more convinced that Germany has faced unique benefits and challenges that differ fundamentally from any other EU country. Its position reflects those realities as well as national interests.

Geography and history matter. As much as modern model-driven economics assumes stationary and ergodic processes, the roll of the dice "at the beginning of time" frequently raises its ugly head at the most inconvenient moments. As stressed by Feldstein (1997a, b, 2011), Europeans refer to their own national histories, and their children are educated in a national perspective. The same nationalism that drove the French Revolution, German Unification, and the Italian Risorgimento can resist or even throttle efficiency gains of deeper economic integration. Wilhelm Röpke (1899–1966), one of the intellectual fathers of German ordoliberalism and the social market economy, warned repeatedly of dangers of nationalism in conjunction with rising imperfect competition and the emergence of national cartels.[1] The rise of the nation-states in the nineteenth century probably cultivated economic integration within nations, but stunted it across political boundaries. The rise of national champions is a poor substitute for international product market competition.

Despite its fragmented and feudal past, Germany's role as a doormat of Europe—a term normally reserved for Poland in the modern setting (A'Barrow 2016)—is a defining element of its history. Centrality is advantageous to the extent that trade routes spanning trading areas intersect at the doormat, as they did in Cologne, Frankfurt, Görlitz, Leipzig, and Magdeburg. Yet the early economic advantages from controlling and taxing these points made it difficult for the nation-state to emerge. While Italian city-states with their water-borne freedom thrived on the gains from international trade, the Holy Roman Empire (962–1806) required centuries to evolve to a customs union (Zollverein 1834), following the urging of Friedrich List, ultimately implemented by Bismarck's "blood and iron" strategy.[2] Having achieved unification, Germany's economic ascent was a combination of innovation, dynamic capitalism, and shrewd social policy. Naturally, intense rivalries with and fears of France, Britain, Russia, and other countries led to spectacular setbacks, despite subsequent recoveries.

Doormat status affords distinct advantages and disadvantages. For Herbert Giersch (1921–2010), the advantage of centrality was not only increasing returns to economic activity (Giersch 1949), but to the innovation process itself, the generation and cross-pollination of ideas that resulted from that function (Giersch 1979).[3] Giersch had spent time at the London School of Economics after the war and had unusual international exposure for his age cohort.[4] In Giersch (1949) he appealed to economic geography inspired by Thünen's (1826) rings—concentric circles describing the economic rents from agglomeration in "isolated cities." Later, Samuelson (1983) would sort out the math, but Giersch had the vision, combined with a sharp intuition, an excellent command of economic history and ideas, and a healthy disrespect for formal methods. Later, Giersch (1979, 2007) would envision Thünen's economic geography in three dimensions, as a volcano—with Düsseldorf at the epicenter! Critical mass and especially Schumpeterian innovation are a key part of Giersch's story—in essence, a spatial version of Romer (1990).

Giersch was chairman of the Council of Economic Advisors (*Sachverständigenrat*) from 1964 to 1970, and had considerable influence on German economic policymaking at the time. He was a somewhat unconventional liberal (in the European sense of the word), a staunch advocate of flexible exchange rates and deregulation who later opposed the euro, signing a manifesto in 1992 with 61 other German economists that would anticipate many of the problems that would later arise. He was responsible for the term *Eurosklerose* (Eurosclerosis) to characterize the continent's mediocre economic performance in the 1980s— Germany's in particular. Giersch was hardly a dogmatic *Ordnungspolitiker*, but an eclectic consumer of Marshall, Keynes, von Mises, Hayek, and, of course, Schumpeter. He was convinced that "Schumpeter-goods"—produced intensively with human capital, innovative freedom, and entrepreneurial talent—were the true engine of technological change and economic progress. He was adamantly critical of all restrictions on innovation, including those due to large corporations, trade unions, international combines, as well as bureaucratic governments.

3.4 When Does European Integration Reach an Inflection Point? The German View

Assessing the German perspective on European integration is no trivial task. The economy has undoubtedly benefited from its doormat-and-volcano status. The pressure of competition from low-wage neighbors both to the east and the west has forced restructuring of both the ex-communist East and the euro-sclerotic West. The influx of cheap imports, intermediate inputs, and immigrant labor, and the exodus of capital (mirrored by chronic current account surpluses) forced institutional reforms in the early 2000s that are now being adopted in France, Italy, and elsewhere. For better or for worse, German labor unions have become more pragmatic, labor markets more flexible, and product markets more liberalized. With an export share of GDP hovering just under 50%, Germans have come to understand the benefits to product and factor market integration, moving them significantly to the pro-globalization end of the spectrum of national opinion in Fig. 3.1. Yet within Europe, Germany's hyper-competitiveness has led to chronic current account surpluses with the volcano's periphery, a source of FDI finance there for many decades.[5]

Figure 3.2 is a stylized depiction of the European economic integration process. One end of the continuum is complete autarky in goods, capital, and labor markets, a hallmark of Europe's regions and nations through much of its history. Trade, especially in finished products, is the lowest hanging fruit, later extended to key intermediate inputs as the advantages of sourcing are discovered. As mutual trust and recognition of civil law

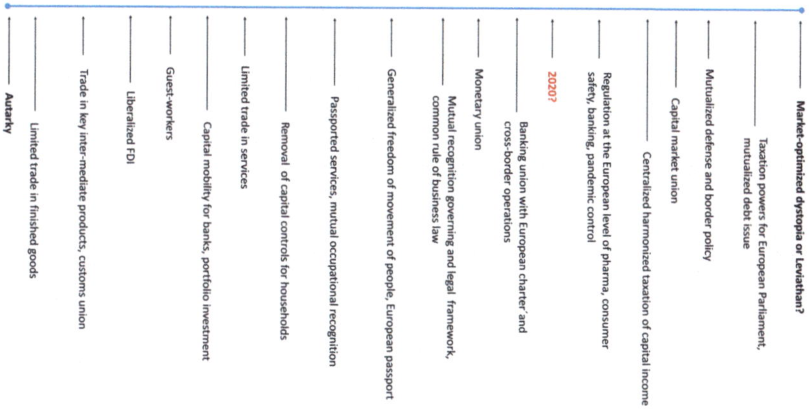

Fig. 3.2 Phases of globalization, or European integration. (Color figure online)

deepen, capital mobility (bank lending, FDI) ensues, followed by trade in services, some tied to people, leading first to temporary, then permanent labor mobility. With generalized mobility of people, ideas, governance frameworks, harmonized standards of justice, and rule of law are bound to follow. Demands for stable exchange rates and a common medium of payment lead to pressure for a common currency, harmonization of financial regulation, and capital market union. This in turn raises issues of taxation, tax collection, and revenue sharing. Fiscal union cannot be far away; social insurance and common taxation lead to explicit supranational political powers, which are better equipped to take shared decisions over thorny issues of externalities, regulation, and subsidization. The terminus is the greatest imaginable degree of product specialization, labor and capital mobility, and cultural and linguistic homogenization. This extreme is unlikely to be acceptable or attainable by any European people; it is natural to expect the inflection point to occur well in advance.

Despite recent trends in modeling social cohesion and fragmentation, economists tend to neglect local identity and cultural heterogeneity when studying European integration, as it is a concession that the representative agent paradigm does not get it quite right. Yet heterogeneity of tastes has long been an issue for the nations of Europe—evidenced by the resounding rejection of a United States of Europe, despite the staggering devastation incurred in WWII. After all, how could Europe possibly speak with one voice, when de Gaulle despaired of consensus in his own fractious country with its 246 varieties of cheese?[6] It is this loss of regional and national identity that weighs heavily on European souls in their quest for identity in the age of globalization. Langella and Manning (2018) document that even tolerant Britons have suffered from perceptions of alienation, change, and loss of satisfaction with their local surroundings. Indeed, among EU countries polled at the time, only Austria had lower approval of EU mobility than the United Kingdom (Bertelsmann Foundation, 2017).

Economic integration has limits evident even in the liberal and open societies of the Nordic countries. In Germany, political discussion—reflected in the rise of the right-wing, anti-immigrant, and populist party AfD (*Alternative für Deutschland*)—suggests that marginal net benefits of integration are no longer evident to the *representative* German, or to the representative loser. As liberal economists, who are we to criticize these sentiments? Are they not simply a recognition that further globalization does not yield the greatest good for the greatest number? Evidently, the regionally and nationally skewed distribution of sentiments reflects a failure of "a rising tide to lift all boats." Schumpeterian dynamics are important for moving forward, yet generalized growth as a dynamo for deeper integration has fallen into disrepute. Mere management of demand and coordinating monetary and fiscal policy is not sufficient to generate sustainable gains for the population.

The EU's greatest failure remains its parlous image in the eyes of its own citizens, even in countries that have benefited the most from membership *on average*. In contrast, the United States, besides being able to reinvent itself at the turn of the hat, is a master of self-promotion. The Declaration of Independence (1776) and Bill of Rights (1789) are the trademark of the American Dream, even though universal suffrage and rights for all genders and races are only a recent reality. The EU has been remarkably unable to sell economic gains from trade, mutual provision of public goods and coordinated solutions to externalities. In a world of heightened factor mobility and cheap communication, the opportunity costs of borders based on cultural, linguistic, or religious origins are high, as the United Kingdom will soon learn.

The failure to market the gains from European economic integration is most evident in the "Four Freedoms," implicit in the Treaty of Rome but made explicit in the Treaty of Maastricht (1992). In his own famous "Four Freedoms" State of the Union Address of January 6, 1941—11 months before Pearl Harbor—US President Franklin Delano Roosevelt spoke of the freedom of speech, the freedom to worship, the freedom from want, and the freedom from fear. This speech would capture the hearts of the American public and prepare them for WWII. In contrast, the Maastricht agenda speaks to four technocratic liberties remarkably devoid of European tradition: free movement of goods, capital, services, and people. The EU "four freedoms" are an egregiously business-friendly proposition. Curiously, there has been no effort to sell these ideas, or expand them, for example, to freedom from bureaucratic burdens when starting an enterprise, or the freedom from government intrusion.

Of the EU's "four freedoms," labor mobility is the most contentious, and most negatively associated with globalization, as Fig. 3.3 shows. This is undoubtedly because Europeans are immobile, a consistent finding in macroeconometric studies of regional employment (e.g., Decressin and Fatás 1995; Fatás 2000; Arpaia et al. 2014). Being a doormat and volcano of Europe is certainly not an easy role for Germany, and eking out a stock of cultural, linguistic, and social capital under these circumstances is likely to create suspicion if not hostility toward outsiders who do not similarly value that capital. The freedom of people to move freely has become more tenuous since the arrival of the coronavirus in February 2020, but was already under siege after the arrival of Syrian immigrants in 2015. European ideas pioneered and promoted by Monnet, Schuman, and Churchill, later Werner and Delors, are increasingly seen as benefiting an elite interested only in its own gains, and labor mobility as a mechanism for raising the profitability of labor-intensive production, rather than increasing consumer surplus for the general populace. It is plausible that the Syrian refugee crisis and Germany's unilateral handling of it ultimately led to Brexit.[7]

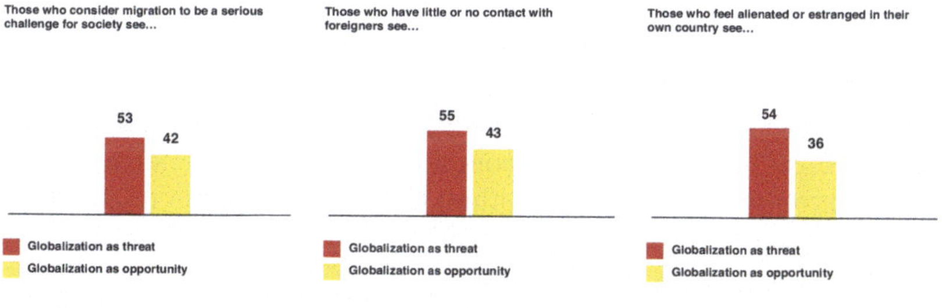

Fig. 3.3 European attitudes toward globalization. (*Source*: de Vries and Hoffmann [2016])

3.5 Conclusion

As my informal survey of conference participants confirmed, few Europeans are aware that the official motto of the European Union is "*In varietate concordia*"—united in diversity. Yet the lack of a single view from the continent is precisely the paradox that unifies—and speaks for a federalist rather than a centralist approach to integration. In Europe, there is no such thing as a representative agent. *Et c'est bien comme ça.* Recognizing heterogeneity and national interests are both a binding and bonding constraint on European integration. Europe must embrace and celebrate that diversity, not suppress it.

Despite its centrality as doormat and volcano, German hegemony faces a fate similar to the Italian city-states, the Hanseatic League, the Kingdom of France, or the British Empire. With transitions underway to new technologies and environmentally sustainable products and production, the economic epicenter of Europe may well move from Düsseldorf or Stuttgart to Eastern Germany and Western Poland, or to back to Italy, or elsewhere. As transport costs rebound from unsustainably low levels, gains from centrality will diminish and competing Schumpeterian volcanoes will emerge. Europe must learn to manage this new form of competition—as well as future gains and losses from re- or disintegration—in a systematic but decentralized way.

Germany is unlikely to relinquish its hegemonic position without an (economic) fight. This position is consistent with a view I have formulated elsewhere (Burda 2017) that German *Ordnungspolitik* is simply an expression of particular national interest: A healthy dose of free market economics and liberalism, *comme ça convient.* These interests originate in German geography and history, as well sociology. Herbert Giersch was fond of describing economics as an undersupplied public good. As economists, we have the job of shining an objective, but merciless spotlight on these contradictions between national interests and economic welfare.

Tim Marshall (2015) writes that the modern world, for better or for worse, springs from Europe. Its paramount challenge in this century will be to protect its precious gains from integration from the forces of deglobalization from without and within. Given the European tribal reflex, the movement of people needs a marketing makeover before the next Brexit occurs. Europe is not a melting pot, but a mosaic. Its elites must devise ways to compensate the losers from integration, especially labor mobility, and better market the "four freedoms" as principles of economic self-realization for all Europeans, a truly liberal idea. An inspirational message to justify these principles will be essential for the survival of the EU in the light of the inevitable retrenchment ahead of us.

Notes

1. See Röpke (1937). I am grateful to Stefan Kolev for drawing my attention to Röpke's fascinating life and *oeuvre*.
2. This German dilemma was described by Bismarck in 1862: "The position of Prussia in Germany will not be determined by its liberalism but by its power … Prussia must concentrate its strength and hold it for the favorable moment, which has already come and gone several times. Since the treaties of Vienna, our frontiers have been ill-designed for a healthy body politic. Not through speeches and majority decisions will the great questions of the day be decided—that was the great mistake of 1848 and 1849 [the German revolutions]—but by iron and blood" (Schüßler 1928, pp. 139–40).
3. Johann Heinrich von Thünen (1783–1850) and Alfred Weber (1868–1958) are responsible for the role of location and "locational competition" (*Standortwettbewerb*) in German economic thought. After Thünen, Weber (1909), Christaller (1933) and Lösch (1940) and others pursued the formal analysis of space and economics. For an overview, see Plehwe and Slobodian (2019).
4. Following the surrender of his submarine at the end of WWII, Giersch spent a year in a British prisoner-of-war camp, where he read *Wealth of Nations* and taught the principles of economics to fellow prisoners. He later came to the London School of Economics in 1948–49 as a Fellow of the British Council (Giersch 1986).
5. After 2010 all that changed, with the TARGET-2 System taking over the financing of intra-European imbalances of payments, with little pressure for adjustment, exposing a flaw in the ECB's setup and creating another intra-European source of tension.
6. «*Comment voulez-vous gouverner un pays qui a deux cent quarante-six variétés de fromage?*» (Mignon 1962, p. 34).
7. It would be simplistic to call this xenophobia. According to the Eurobarometer 86 conducted in fall 2016—an EU-wide survey of more than 27,000 people—82% of Europeans "were in favor of EU citizens having the freedom to live, work, study, and do business anywhere in the EU" (Bertelsmann Foundation 2017). Consistent with this view, individual countries exhibit significant variability, with patterns consistent with those in Fig. 3.1.

References

A'Barrow, Stephen. 2016. *Death of a Nation: A New History of Germany*. Hove: Book Guild Publishing.

Arpaia, Alfonso, Aron Kiss, Balasz Palvolgyi, and Alessandro Turrini. 2014. *Labour mobility and labor market adjustment in the EU*. European Economy Economic Papers 539. Brussels: European Commission Directorate-General for Economic and Financial Affairs.

Baldwin, Richard E., and Charles Wyplosz. 2019. *The Economics of European Integration*. London: McGraw-Hill.

Barro, Robert J., and Xavier Sala-i-Martin. 1991. Convergence. *Journal of Political Economy* 100: 223–251. Chicago: University of Chicago Press.

———. 1992. Convergence Across States and Regions. *Brookings Papers of Economic Activity* 22: 107–182. Washington, DC: Brookings Institution.

Bertelsmann Foundation, and Jacques-Delors-Institute Berlin. 2017. *The Four Freedoms in the EU: Are They Inseparable?* Gütersloh: Bertelsmann Stiftung.

Burda, Michael C. 2017. Ordnungsökonomik or Teutonomik? In *Ordoliberalism: A German oddity?* ed. Thorsten Beck and Hans-Helmut Kotz, 53–62. London: Centre for Economic Policy Research.

Christaller, Walter. 1933. *Die zentralen Orte in Süddeutschland. Eine ökonomisch-geographische Untersuchung über die Gesetzmässigkeit der Verbreitung und Entwicklung der Siedlungen mit städtischen Funktionen*. Jena: Gustav Fischer.

Decressin, Jörg, and Antonio Fatás. 1995. Regional Labor Market Dynamics in Europe. *European Economic Review* (9): 1627–1655.

Eichengreen, Barry. 1990. One Money for Europe? Lessons from the US Currency Union. *Economic Policy* (10): 118–187.

Fatás, Antonio. 2000. Intranational Migration: Business Cycles and Growth. In *Intranational Macroeconomics*, ed. Gregory D. Hess and Eric van Wincoop, 156–188. Cambridge: Cambridge University Press.

Feenstra, Robert. 2003. *Advanced International Trade*. Princeton, NJ: Princeton University Press.

Feldstein, Martin. 1997a. EMU and International Conflict. *Foreign Affairs* 76: 60–73.

———. 1997b. The Political Economy of the European Economic and Monetary Union: Political Sources of an Economic Liability. *Journal of Economic Perspectives* 11: 23–42.

———. 2011. *The Euro and European Economic Conditions*. NBER Working Paper, 17617. Cambridge, MA: National Bureau of Economic Research.

Giersch, Herbert. 1949. Economic Union between Nations and the Location of Industries. *Review of Economic Studies* 17: 87–97.

———. 1979. Aspects of Growth, Structural Change, and Employment–A Schumpeterian Perspective. *Weltwirtschaftliches Archiv* 115: 629–652.

———. 1986. L'economia come bene pubblico. *Banca Nazionale del Lavoro Quarterly Review* 156: 251–273.

———. 2007. Lösch's Message—in a World Economics Perspective. In *Space-Structure-Economy: A Tribute to August Lösch*, ed. Ulrich Blum, Rolf Funck, Jan Kowalski, Antoni Kuklinski, and Werner Rothengatter, 81–99. Baden-Baden: Nomos.

Johnson, Harry G. 1971. Problems of European Monetary Union. *Journal of World Trade Law* 4: 377–387.

Langella, Monica, and Alan Manning. 2018. Diversity and Neighborhood Satisfaction. *The Economic Journal* 129: 3219–3255.

Lösch, August. 1940. *Die Räumliche Ordnung der Wirtschaft. Eine Untersuchung über Standort, Wirtschaftsgebiete und internationalen Handel.* Jena: Gustav Fischer.

Marshall, Tim. 2015. *Prisoners of Geography: Ten Maps That Tell You Everything You Need to Know About Global Politics.* London: Elliott&Thompson.

Mignon, Ernest. 1962. *Les Mots du Général De Gaulle.* Paris: Fayard.

Mundell, Robert A. 1957. International Trade and Factor Mobility. *American Economic Review* 47: 321–335.

———. 1961. A Theory of Optimum Currency Areas. *American Economic Review* 4: 657–665.

Plehwe, Dieter, and Quinn Slobodian. 2019. Landscapes of Unrest: Herbert Giersch and the Origins of Liberal Economic Geography. *Modern Intellectual History* (1): 185–215.

Romer, Paul M. 1990. Endogenous Technological Change. *Journal of Political Economy* 98: 71–102.

Röpke, Wilhelm. 1937. *Die Lehre von der Wirtschaft.* Vienna: Springer.

Samuelson, Paul A. 1983. Thünen at Two Hundred. *Journal of Economic Literature* 4: 1468–1488.

Schüßler, Wilhelm ed. 1928. Reden 1847–1869. In *Bismarck: Die gesammelten Werke [Bismarck: Collected Works]*, vol. 10. Berlin: Otto Stolberg.

Solow, Robert M. 1956. A Contribution to the Theory of Economic Growth. *Quarterly Journal of Economics* 70: 65–94.

Swan, Trevor W. 1956. Economic Growth and Capital Accumulation. *Economic Record* 32: 334–361.

Thünen, Johann Heinrich. 1826. *Der isoli[e]rte Staat in Beziehung auf Landwirtschaft und Nationalökonomie.* Hamburg: Perthes.

de Vries, Catherine, and Isabelle Hoffmann. 2016. *Globalisierungsangst oder Wertekonflikt? Wer in Europa populistische Parteien wählt und warum.* Gütersloh: Bertelsmann Stiftung.

Weber, Alfred. 1909. *Über den Standort der Industrien. Erster Teil. Reine Theorie des Standorts.* Tübingen: Mohr.

CHAPTER 4

The European "Postwar Consensus" and the Birth of the EEC

Richard Portes

Ideas are at least as important as facts, and indeed ideas often shape or even create facts. I say this not only because of the title of our conference. Partly it is my *deformation professionelle* as an academic, partly my current macroprudential policy role, where I do see academic thinking strongly influencing policy. But I believe you will see it too in the remarks that follow on the background to the birth of the European Economic Community (EEC). One theme here is the intellectual background of federalism. Some say now that European federalist ideas have fallen by the wayside. But I believe that even a Europe of concentric circles would not discard federalist notions—especially with the eurozone at its center.

The "postwar consensus" often appears simply as Franco-German rapprochement with some help from the United States through NATO. But that ignores Italy's role, which was important especially in developing the ideology of European unification. Without any exaggeration, I would

R. Portes (✉)
London Business School, London, UK

CEPR, London, UK
e-mail: rportes@london.edu

F. Giavazzi et al. (eds.), *The Liberal Heart of Europe*,
https://doi.org/10.1007/978-3-030-60368-7_4

argue that Italy played a major part in the thinking leading up to the EEC. Of course, Jean Monnet and Robert Schuman were major figures—though Monnet's original vision was quite different. The conventional story also gives little attention to the role of the United States, which was key in the realization of federalist ideas.

4.1 The Italians

To understand the Italian contribution, one must go back to pre-war and wartime thought. At the center was a liberal socialism, or social liberalism. I should stress that this was very clearly market-based. Carlo Rosselli was a key figure, and before him Piero Gobetti and others. They were convinced of the complementarity of domestic liberal socialism and European federalism (though not all the federalists were liberal socialists—e.g., Luigi Einaudi). Rosselli was assassinated by Mussolini's thugs in 1937, but the vision animated the Manifesto of Ventotene, *For a free and united Europe*, written mainly by Altiero Spinelli (Spinelli and Rossi 1941). He was then further left.

The manifesto became the program of the Movimento Federalista Europeo:

> The dividing line between progressive and reactionary parties no longer follows the formal line of greater or lesser democracy, or of more or less socialism ... [We stand with] those who see the creation of a solid international state as the main purpose ... having won power, will use it first and foremost as an instrument for achieving international unity. (Spinelli and Rossi 1941, pp. 32–3)

In 1943, Ernesto Rossi wrote *Gli Stati Uniti d'Europa* (Storeno 1944). In January 1945, the Rector of the University of Florence spoke at the first congress of the European Federalist Society. The Action Party founded in January 1943 combined the views of Rosselli and Guido Calogero. In its program, Italy was to be a secular, republican state within a European federation. But it never had a mass base—it was a party of intellectuals, at heart.

That is why Spinelli was so important: he became an active politician, a member of the European Commission for several years, and a highly influential advocate of federalism as opposed to the intergovernmental approach. His influence can be seen in the Single European Act of 1986 and the Maastricht Treaty. (His turn away from Communism and Togliatti's turn away from the Soviets were key in reducing the influence of the Communist Party, which was for some years a great concern of the Americans.)

Still, there was a rejection of the Italian idealistic vision in Italy itself. The Action Party did name the first postwar prime minister, Ferruccio Parri, who had been in Lipari with Rosselli. But he fell in five months, too weak to resist the Church and the Christian Democrats (CD). Alcide De Gasperi took over, and the CD were in power for the following 46 years. The idea of European federalism moved out of the mainstream. But it was still influential in the background.

4.2 The Americans

The key American aim was to restart the German economy. This was the main thrust of the Marshall Plan, which also led to the Organization for European Economic Cooperation. The OEEC's initial purpose was to administer the Marshall Plan. It then became the OECD that we have today. But note the name itself, which shifts the emphasis away from American aid to individual countries toward "European economic cooperation."

The underlying motivation, and the main argument used to sell the program politically in the US, was anti-Communism: countering the Soviet threat and fostering West European cohesion in the face of Soviet control of Eastern Europe. At the heart of the Cold War was the Soviet-US conflict over what to do about Germany.

US policy was clear, and American support of German economic regeneration was a powerful force in leading France to embrace economic coordination as a means of containing German economic power. Note that Monnet immediately after the war was an economic nationalist, advocating French control of the Ruhr. Then his position changed.

4.3 France and Germany

We know this story well. The War discredited the idea of the sovereign, all-powerful nation-state, which had been a dominant theme in Fascism. France focused on limiting German power—and this fits well with what some have called a German "leadership avoidance complex" (Paterson 1996), turning 180 degrees away from Hitlerian notions of domination.

The obvious solution was to put Germany together with France at the center of an economically integrated unit. And France saw economic integration as a way of taking some control over German policy. (Compare the motivation for the single currency—France was frustrated with having to follow the Bundesbank's monetary policy without any influence on it.) Note that this thinking had very little to do with the view that trade creates friends—to which there are many counterexamples.

That said, there was a significant component of idealistic supranational federalism, as propounded by Schuman. He was already talking of Franco-German reconciliation early in the War, though he was suspect because of his early though brief participation in the Petain government. In 1948, as Prime Minister, he proposed plans for the Council of Europe and the principles of a Single Market. The Schuman Declaration of 1949 put all this most eloquently.

The beginning, the European Coal and Steel Community, was a "lowest common denominator." Monnet's federalism was based on a sequence of small steps.

Again, the security/geopolitical dimension was important: the French saw they were too small to influence the United States or the USSR alone. But the developments in the 1950s were dominated by economics and, in particular, by the perceived advantages of economic integration.

This went further than a trade-off of support for French agriculture in exchange for markets for German industry. Beyond the customs union and the unique Community competence in trade policy, a key feature of the Treaty of Rome—perhaps surprisingly—was the creation of a robust framework for a unique Community competence in competition policy. That included not only anti-cartel policy, but also a bar against state aids (government subsidies to individual firms). This has become increasingly important, for example, in dealing with financial institution bailouts during and after the financial crisis. Competition policy, under a succession of outstanding Commissioners who gradually brought economic analysis together with the excessively legal approach of the early years, has endured as one of the most effective and best managed elements of European economic integration. This was independently of (though partly influenced by) the German *Kartellamt*. The contrast with the demise of American antitrust is striking.

Sadly, however, this remarkable achievement is under threat today from both France and Germany. Do they want to permit both state aids and anti-competitive mergers, the latter in the face of considerable evidence that firm size per se is a negative influence on productivity and innovation? Surely if competition policy becomes intergovernmental, subject to the Council, there can be no doubt we shall move to "anything goes." This would be a major step backward in European integration.

References

Paterson, William E. 1996. Beyond Semi-Sovereignty. The New Germany in the New Europe. *German Politics* 2: 167–184.

Spinelli, Altiero, and Ernesto Rossi. (1941) 1988. *Towards a Free and United Europe: A Manifesto*. Ventotene: Altiero Spinelli Institute for Federalist Studies.

Storeno. 1944. *Gli stati uniti d'Europa: introduzione allo studio del problema*. Lugano: Nuove Edizioni Capolago.

CHAPTER 5

"Large Switzerland" or "Large France"? The Ordoliberals and Early European Integration

Stefan Kolev

5.1 Introduction: Two Visions of Europe

For the process of European integration, the past decade has been above all a sequence of cumulative crises. The combined effects of the financial, Eurozone, Crimea, refugee, and Brexit crises stifled much of the earlier optimism about the quasi-automatic formation of an "ever closer union." The current struggle with the consequences of the coronavirus has produced yet another stress test for the architecture of the European Union, especially regarding the basic freedoms when borders are being closed and unprecedented restrictive measures in the public space are being introduced, but also regarding the problem-solving capacities for this new macroeconomic shock on the national and supranational levels.

This chapter focuses on the early phase in the process of European integration as seen from the perspective of the German political economists

S. Kolev (✉)
University of Applied Sciences Zwickau, Zwickau, Germany
e-mail: stefan.kolev@fh-zwickau.de

F. Giavazzi et al. (eds.), *The Liberal Heart of Europe*,
https://doi.org/10.1007/978-3-030-60368-7_5

whose combination of the notions of liberty and order led to the designation "ordoliberalism." Special attention is given to Wilhelm Röpke (1899–1966) who accompanied the first decades of the integration process as theorist and public intellectual. The positions of Ludwig Erhard (1897–1977) and Alfred Müller-Armack (1901–1978) are incorporated to provide the political perspective in the complex negotiations leading to the Treaty of Rome. Since for many protagonists the early phase of European integration was motivated by the central aim to contain the young West German Federal Republic and to integrate its war-relevant industries into a common entity, the positions of these three German political economists in their different roles are of particular interest. As theorists, public intellectuals, and policymakers, they were formative not only for the decision-making process in Germany, but also for the observers in neighboring countries and for reassuring them. Overall, the narrative centers around a key metaphor of two visions of Europe that helps to structure these early debates: For the ordoliberals, the trajectories of European integration could bring about a "large Switzerland," that is, a politically decentralized entity which is economically integrated internally as well as non-protectionist externally, or a "large France," that is, a politically centralized entity which is economically integrated internally but protectionist externally. From today's perspective, this prescient diagnosis is not only of historical value: While it is instrumental to capture the oscillations of European integration between the two trajectories during the past seven decades, it is also conducive to therapies for the crises-ridden EU of today and tomorrow which, especially in recent decades, has arguably moved toward a "large France."

5.2 Europe's Diverse Faces: From Zeus and Europa to *Festung Europa*

What are the key vehicles for communicating history? Many would reply: books. This is certainly true, at least since the majority of citizens has become functionally literate and thus has the capacity to engage in historical texts. And yet, much earlier than our global-digital age with its new media channels, another vehicle has been very powerful: images. Images are capable of capturing collective imaginations of a phenomenon at a point in time, and correspondingly one can grasp the history of a certain phenomenon as a sequence of such images which has accumulated over time.

In the case of Europe, the power of collective images is very much palpable. A large piece of land as a continent is not necessarily predestined to play an important role in the popular imagination. For this to happen, a set of "mythical and symbolic underpinnings" (Bottici and Challand 2009, p. 11) is required. And Europe has been on the minds of humanity for millennia, captured in a number of principal images: The Greek myth of Europa (Klocek di Blasio and Michalski 2016), the images of ancient Athens and Rome as the cradles of civilization (Spawforth and Walker 1985), the Renaissance as the awakening of Western civilization (Patterson 1997) are prominent examples of such mythical and symbolic underpinnings which are almost universally shared today. In addition to their universal spread, it can be argued that for today's Europeans they invoke mostly positive associations.

However, there is a different type of images of Europe which, even if not universally shared, invoke more controversial associations and less unambiguous emotions. A prominent example here is the historical image of Europe as a patchwork of small states as it presented itself for several centuries prior to the emergence of the nation-state. This pattern persisted particularly long in Central Europe, and until today for many Germans the notion of "*Kleinstaaterei*" (Kamusella 2012, pp. 75–80) is taken as a synonym for fragmentation, weakness of state capacity, and diplomatic irrelevance. In contrast, the counter-interpretation of this "*Kleinstaaterei*" as a realm of diversity where the abundance of small territories provided an essential laboratory for learning through experimentation with various regulatory frameworks for economy and society (Rohac 2019, pp. 53–9) is much less widely shared and more or less confined to the pronouncements of proponents of liberalism.

As an initiation of this narrative of postwar European integration, it is important to ask what dominant images of Europe were on the minds of the generation which is at the core of the chapter. The period 1942–1943 is a suitable anchor to depict two extremes in the spectrum of images. On the one hand, Stefan Zweig's *The World of Yesterday: Memoirs of a European* (Zweig [1942] 1943) was posthumously published shortly after he had committed suicide in Brazil. Zweig's brilliant and section-wise melancholic account of the decline of European civilization since 1914 praised the diversity of European cultures, European solidarity across borders, and cosmopolitanism. On the other hand, in the course of the deterioration of the war situation for the National Socialists, they increasingly invoked the image of *Festung Europa* and attempted to depict the war efforts as being not about Germany but about protecting this fortified Europe against enemies in the East and in the West (Rosenberg 1943; Russell 1944). Given the prominence of the image of a unified Europe under German leadership, which lived through the horrors of such a unified Europe from 1939 to 1945 (Mazower 2008), the initiation of the European unification project so soon after the end of the war can by no means be taken for granted.

5.3 Disintegration Before Integration, Identity Through Friends and Foes

By shedding light on crucial concepts, this section lays the foundation for penetrating the history of the first decades of European integration. The concept "integration," its history, and sources are the natural outset for such a task. Fritz Machlup's *A History of Thought on Economic Integration* (Machlup 1977) proves of invaluable help regarding the usage of "integration" in international economics. Machlup shows how, at least in English, the term was not in circulation until the late 1930s and that curiously it was "disintegration" which first emerged during the 1930s as a scholarly concept to capture the falling apart of the global economy after 1914, especially since the protectionist race of most nations during and after the Great Depression (Machlup 1977, pp. 4–9).

In this literature which was largely produced by European liberal political economists, several of whom were based in Geneva, Machlup emphasized Wilhelm Röpke's contributions and especially his *International Economic Disintegration* (Röpke 1942) as a pioneering work not only in diagnosing this process of interwar disintegration but also in suggesting therapies how this impasse could be overcome after the end of the war. The European pioneer of explicitly using "integration" in English, as identified by Machlup, was the Swedish economist Folke Hilgerdt in his *The Network of World Trade* (Hilgerdt 1942a). The curiosity that the book was officially published in Geneva but actually printed in the US by Princeton University Press due to the move of the League of Nations' Economic Intelligence Service from Geneva to Princeton, along with the publication of US economist John S. De Beers (1941) as well as Hilgerdt's contemporaneous publications (Hilgerdt 1942b, 1943), may have been the conduits across the Atlantic to initiate the usage of "integration" in the US. "Integration" became common parlance in the US, first in bureaucratic documents, during the immediate postwar years (Machlup 1977, pp. 8–12).

A look at the etymology is also illuminating: The Latin *integrare* means not only to put pieces together but also to recreate or renovate something that existed before (Thode 2003, p. 29). The latter meaning is particularly interesting: It adds a nuance that integration is not simply a process open to future outcomes, but also a process that can identify anchors in the past serving as points of orientation (Lachmann 1971, pp. 39–40) that can inspire and guide the unfolding of the cognitive processes in the minds of the players involved. Indeed, what happened in the postwar decades in Europe had predecessors in the past, both in intellectual history and in economic history: Machlup's book identifies a rich set of ideational strands (Machlup 1977, Part II) as well as institutional and personal contributors (Machlup 1977, Part III) on the basis of which his generation thought about integration in the post-WWII decades. For this very generation, the pre-1914 world with its first wave of globalization commonly served as the ideal, both regarding the economic order in the German-speaking world and the types of integration achieved globally in the domains of trade, capital flows, and migration during this first wave of globalization (Wegner 2020a, b).

The motivational forces driving integration are also of interest here, in other words the identity of an integration process: Is such a process primarily motivated by a positive identity targeted at unifying with certain partners, or is it rather a project targeted at unifying against certain adversaries? In the case of early European integration, three patterns can be identified: integration against the increasing threats from the Soviet Union (Mueller 2009), integration with Western European partners, and integration with the US as an ally (Jarausch 2015). When studying different proponents and phases of European integration, different combinations of these three patterns are discernible, from the Marshall Plan until today. In the larger history of Europe's identity—from the ancient Greeks over the Middle Ages to the Enlightenment—intellectual history shows that identity has been very often drawn from a distinction against adversaries captured through the notion of "the Other," commonly equated to the notion of "barbarians" (Salter 2002, pp. 18–21). In this distinction, "the East" as embodied by Russia—from the Muscovy over the Tsarist centuries to the Soviet Union—played a formative part of "the Other" as an adversary (Neumann 1999, pp. 67–112), while "the West" as embodied by the US transformed into a formative part of "the Other" as an ally (Larres 1999, pp. 83–6). The increasing aggression of the Soviet Union in the immediate postwar years which culminated in the Berlin Blockade of 1948–1949 (Murphy et al. 1997), and, after some initial indecisiveness, the increasing commitment of the US in Western Europe culminating in the Marshall Plan of 1947 (Bissell et al. 1996) provided the geopolitical framework. And within this framework, Western European scholars and politicians made the first steps toward "integrating" the pieces of the continent, which had economically belonged together before 1914 and yet had politically consisted of adversaries for centuries.

5.4 Wilhelm Röpke as a Theorist of (Dis-)Integration

The central figure of this chapter is the German political economist Wilhelm Röpke (1899–1966) and that for a number of reasons. To begin with, in the 1920s he had already written on those international economics intricacies which, along with the hyperinflation and the Great Depression, seriously hindered the Weimar Republic's prosperity. In 1937, after four years of exile in Istanbul, he received a call to the Institut Universitaire de Hautes Études Internationales (HEI) in Geneva (Frachebourg 2002) and lived until his passing in one of the most internationalist cities in the world—amid the bleakness of looming military conflicts in Europe. Röpke was hired at HEI with the assignment to identify diagnoses for the disintegration of the post-1914 global economy and therapies for its reconstruction (Hennecke 2005, pp. 111–4; Slobodian 2018, pp. 73–6). The spirit of Geneva and of the HEI, his specific assignment, as well as the luxury of living outside Germany in those darkest years of Central Europe meant that Röpke was uniquely privileged—especially when compared to his like-minded colleagues who remained in Germany, above all the Freiburg School around Walter Eucken, and Alexander Rüstow, who remained in the peripheral Istanbul (Kolev 2019a, pp. xix–xxiii). Correspondingly, out of the group of political economists who would become known as the ordoliberals in the postwar years, Röpke was the scholar who could—and did—dedicate a particular amount of his intellectual energy to the problems of international economics.

As outlined in the previous section, the question of the future of Western Europe became a pressing issue very soon during the immediate postwar years, and Röpke had laid the conceptual foundations for bringing together what had successively fallen apart since 1914. Already during the war, he published *International Economic Disintegration* with William Hodge in London (Röpke 1942) as the outcome of his HEI assignment. The book distinguished different levels of disintegration. Apart from the empirical investigation of the agrarianization of industrial countries and the industrialization of agricultural countries as a result of the disturbances in the global division of labor, a crucial Röpkean distinction was the one between economic and extra-economic disintegration. In his view, economic disintegration consisted of the emergence of protectionism conducted by isolated economic blocs and bilateralism, the destruction of the gold standard as the overarching monetary system, and the hindrance of the flows of factors of production due to proliferating practices of economic nationalism. Even more important for the long-term reintegration of the pre-1914 order was the process of extra-economic disintegration: It led to the exhaustion of "certain psycho-moral reserves" (Röpke 1942, p. 69) that were needed as ideational prerequisites for the market economy to thrive, but in Röpke's theory those prerequisites were not produced by the market economy itself. It is to those extra-economic prerequisites and preconditions that Röpke dedicated the first two volumes of his wartime trilogy, *The Social Crisis of Our Time* ([1942] 1950) and *Civitas Humana* ([1944] 1948), while the third volume, *International Order and Economic Integration* ([1945] 1959), emphasized the economic processes of disintegration and integration. Röpke was convinced that both of these levels, the economic and the extra-economic, had to be thought as being interdependent and as forming an "*ordre public international*" (Warneke 2013, pp. 36–44), or else the challenges of rebuilding the ruins of Europe could not be solved sustainably.

Ordoliberalism is often understood as a system of political economy formulated on the basis of principles (Rieter and Zweynert 2010; Kolev 2019b; Dold and Krieger 2020), and thus it is appropriate to start with Röpke's five principles regarding the future of economic and extra-economic integration of Europe (Petersen and Wohlgemuth 2010, pp. 207–17): (1) endorsing pre-1914 Europe as the ideal of post-WWII integration, that is, interdependence of markets, multilateralism, international monetary system, no prohibitive tariffs, free movement of capital and people; (2) conducting ordoliberal economic policies on the national and lower levels as the prerequisite for integration, that is, focusing integration on the principles of federalism, subsidiarity, and decentralism; (3) enabling the convertibility of national currencies; (4) abandoning central planning on the national level; and (5) discarding "economism," that is, not limiting integration to the economic level and avoiding the neglect of cultural prerequisites for integration beyond economics and politics.

Röpke's five principles add up to a roadmap both for national economic policies and for the necessary steps to initiate and sustain integration of potential national partners. An additional question is posed by the political forms into which those five principles can be sustainably implemented. For these political forms, Röpke's notion of "true internationalism" is of special relevance, that is, the belief that Europe's diversity can only be preserved if—in contrast to the negative reading of *Kleinstaaterei* outlined in Sect. 5.2—integration classifies this historical heritage of diversity as an asset and finds forms to capitalize on it (Sally 1994, pp. 470–4). Such a position emphasizes the principle of subsidiarity, and Röpke's own notion of subsidiarity and decentralism profited from his exchange with representatives of Catholic social teaching and their notion of subsidiarity formulated in the pontifical encyclicals: "It is gravely wrong to take from individuals what they can accomplish by their own initiative and industry and give it to the community. It is also an injustice, grave evil and a disturbance of right order to assign to a greater and a higher association what a lesser and subordinate organization can do" (Pius XI 1931, paragraph 79).

In this worldview, trust in the individual, one's natural embeddedness in small decentralized units, and the problem-solving capacities of such units are able to capture Europe's uniqueness (Kenney 1955; Warneke 2013, pp. 44–7). And it is on those lower levels where integration must start: "European disintegration, like charity in the English proverb, began at home, and the reintegration of Europe's economy must likewise begin at home, i.e. within each individual nation" (Röpke [1945] 1959, p. 228). If the nation-state featured in Röpke's five principles, this happened for pragmatic reasons, given the nation-state's being the principal arena of democratic deliberation of the age:

> [...] the nation in its political organization is partly too large and partly too small. Too large for the evolution of genuinely free and neighbourly communal life and for true and permanent integration, which is able to exist without degenerating into nationalistic self-intoxication of mass-consciousness. Too small for those intellectual, political and economic

> relations which today can only flourish satisfactorily in an international community. (Röpke [1945] 1959, p. 45)

This set of principles of economic and political integration are elegantly captured in juxtaposing the future trajectories of Europe as becoming a "large Switzerland" or a "large France," and Röpke clearly sympathized with the former. Two quotations are particularly illuminating. When discarding the notion of the European "superstate," he diagnosed:

> There is unanimity today among socialists and nonsocialists that the unification of European nations to an international government is at best possible in the loose form of a federation similar to the Swiss Confederation which is preserving the national specificities [...] this federation can only exist if its economic ordering principle is, like in the case of the Swiss Confederation, that of a market economy and not that of a bureaucratic economy. (Röpke 1951, pp. 288–9)

as well as

> This ideal of a centralist nation which arose in the past following the pattern of France must be overcome, but not through new continental nationalism and centralism, but instead through a form of unification which corresponds to the spirit of Europe. This form is federalism which, following the pattern of Switzerland, is the only one which is able to realize unity in diversity. (Röpke [1958] 2009, p. 238)

If the evolution of European integration is depicted as oscillating between those two trajectories of a "large Switzerland" or a "large France," Röpke had a self-understanding beyond that of an analyst of these possibilities. For him, "political economy" was not only the traditional name of economics. Rather, political economists had the obligation to openly express their value judgments about the various goals and ends of political processes (Röpke [1942] 2015; Christ 2018). And early European integration—along with the success of the Social Market Economy in the young Federal Republic—possessed top priority for the political economist Röpke. The next section reconstructs his stance on the concrete steps of integration.

5.5 Wilhelm Röpke as an Activist Observer of Integration

Based on the conceptual foundations and principles outlined above, Röpke became one of the first genuinely European intellectuals on the issues of the continent's economic and political integration. The number of his journalistic interventions in the different languages of European media, all the way from the Marshall Plan and the Schuman Plan to Röpke's passing in 1966, exceeded 150 (Peukert 1992, pp. 1385–93). Already the rapprochement of Jean Monnet and Robert Schuman to France's neighbors and especially to the barely one-year-old Federal Republic did not meet Röpke's enthusiasm, and he expressed his skepticism in similar terms as he had voiced critique of the Marshall Plan (Petersen and Wohlgemuth 2010, pp. 223–4). In the *ORDO Jahrbuch* he depicted the Schuman Plan's focus on integrating the coal and steel industries as a "textbook-like example" of "the economic logic of international central planning" (Röpke 1951, p. 289). First, he assessed this attempt at integrating the essential industries as hardly compatible with the status of most national economies as of 1950, which were not structurally prepared for integration due to the continuous predomination of foreign exchange controls and protectionism, as well as isolationist economic and fiscal policies (Schüller 1950)—policies already identified by Röpke as the hindrance for a long-term success of the Marshall Plan beyond alleviating some short-term hardships. Second, he emphasized his apprehension regarding the coordinating mechanisms endowed by the Schuman Plan to the new "*autorité*" and the likelihood of its management of the coal and steel industries to become a new device of supranational central planning (Röpke 1951, pp. 289–90). At the same time, he expressed his skepticism about the new European Payment Union as proposed in 1950: Like the Marshall Plan and the Schuman Plan, in Röpke's view it would not be conducive to abandoning the underlying structural problems of the national economies, here especially the foreign exchange controls and the non-convertibility of national currencies (Röpke [1952] 1962, p. 180; 1954, p. 78).

On the way to the Treaty of Rome, Röpke remained a skeptic: Neither the European Coal and Steel Community (ECSC) nor the negotiations which in 1957 led to the establishment of the European Communities, especially the European Economic Community (EEC), were received enthusiastically by him (Warneke 2013, pp. 107–19). Röpke opposed the Common Market as embodied by the EEC for a number of reasons. His apprehensions were especially the persisting non-convertibility of the currencies, the potential of the EEC to develop protectionist tendencies toward the rest of the world, and the potential for supranational central planning in the EEC's organs (Röpke 1957, pp. 176–82). All those risks which he attested to the young EEC were assessed by him as much less pronounced in the competing project of the European Free Trade Area (EFTA), and thus Röpke's clear preference for EFTA over EEC: The risk that the EEC could become a protectionist bloc possessed the serious external potential not only to threaten the Transatlantic relations, but also to evolve internally into a centralist political entity which he called the "colossal state" (Röpke [1957] 1958a, pp. 20–21). The tendency toward such a superstate could counteract most of the five principles outlined in Sect. 5.4, resulting in Röpke's succinct warnings about the threats inherent in the EEC. In addition, he warned that EURATOM, as another European Community, could become "the ideal ground for the thriving of a combination of technocracy and economocracy" and thus be captured by experts on the field of technology and economics (Röpke 1958b, p. 31). These experts embodied Röpke's skepticism of centralization in economy and society, while constituting the very opposite to his ideal of integration outlined in Sect. 5.4, an ideal aiming at a political entity constituted by the principles of federalism, subsidiarity, and decentralism. To reproduce Röpke's specific rhetoric contained in these warnings, three of them (many more are contained in Petersen and Wohlgemuth 2010) are reproduced here: "Europe should not become an altar to which the market economy may be sacrificed" (Röpke [1957] 1958a, p. 29), and "What was supposed to be mortar and was praised as such, turned out in reality to be dynamite" (Röpke 1959, p. 88), as well as "It is very difficult for an economist to be a good European and to simultaneously have the reputation of a good European" (Röpke 1955, p. 1).

A final source of apprehension regarding the nature and potential of ECSC and EEC was Röpke's assessment of the relationship of European integration to the General Agreement on Tariffs and Trade (GATT). In a recent widely discussed history of neoliberalism, Röpke is depicted as a principal defender of GATT as the institutional anchor in the postwar world, on which he posed his hopes for a comeback of multilateral international trade in line with his pre-1914 ideal (Slobodian 2018, pp. 182–93). Röpke and the Austrian economist Gottfried Haberler (1900–1995) are depicted in this narrative as "the universalists" whose aim was the establishment of multilateral international trade, so that any regional bloc like the EEC was a threat to multilateral trade due to the aforementioned fears about such blocs' protectionist potential. In contrast, a younger generation of economists and lawyers represented by Erich Hoppmann (1923–2007) and Ernst-Joachim Mestmäcker (*1926), called "the constitutionalists," saw the EEC as a project in which regional integration could be deepened beyond GATT's focus on trade, initially incurring the protectionist potential vis-à-vis the rest of the world, but hoping to later scale up Europe's level of integration to the global level (Slobodian 2018, pp. 202–10).

To summarize these and other pronouncements of Röpke, he can be described as an activist observer who, more than just expressing skepticism, was fighting for his notion of "true internationalism." He saw the potential of integration in overcoming the war-related ruins of foreign exchange controls, non-convertibility, and central planning on the national level by instituting a supranational framework—but of the EFTA, not of the EEC type. He saw the potential of integration to bring European nations together—if the process allowed for the necessary time for cultures to approach each other and slowly create a common identity. He saw the potential of integration for reintroducing market economy principles in line with the pre-1914 order instead of central planning and interventionism—if this process was not conducted top-down by experts aiming at centralization, but instead bottom-up by citizens and federal political units bound by the principles of federalism, subsidiarity, and decentralism. Röpke's overall approach to integration has been succinctly summarized by the motto "liberalism from below" (Sally 1999, pp. 48–51).

5.6 Ludwig Erhard and Alfred Müller-Armack: Functionalist or Institutionalist Integration

This section enhances the picture by introducing two fellow ordoliberals of Röpke who belonged to the same generation and were formative for the process of early European integration. Like Röpke, they were economists by education, and unlike Röpke, during the postwar years, they found a new vocation and primary role, despite academic credentials and continuing publications, in the political domain: Ludwig Erhard (1897–1977) and Alfred Müller-Armack (1901–1978). Once Müller-Armack coined the concept "Social Market Economy" in 1946–1947 (Müller-Armack 1947; Siebert 2005, pp. 24–37), Erhard became the political entrepreneur who, after the June 1948 reforms of introducing the new DM currency and liberalizing numerous prices, became the international symbol of the Social Market Economy as the concept behind the German economic miracle (Erhard 1958, pp. 10–36; Berghahn 2015). Erhard served as minister of the economy of the Federal Republic from 1949 to 1963 and as federal chancellor from 1963 to 1966, while Müller-Armack served as a top official in Erhard's ministry from 1952 to 1963.

When drawing a comparative picture of the different German positions in those first decades of European integration, Erhard and Müller-Armack occupy a curious in-between position, between Röpke on the one hand and the position of the German foreign ministry on the other. Erhard's and Müller-Armack's approaches can be captured by the notion of "functionalist integration," while their foreign ministry colleagues favored "institutionalist integration" (Warneke 2013, pp. 124–5). Essentially, the main difference is the degree of willingness to pass the autonomy of lower political entities in the integration process to overarching institutions, which become increasingly dominant players in this process. Institutionalists show a higher willingness to build such overarching institutions, like the EEC Commission, while functionalists assert that removing interstate hindrances to trade (first-degree integration) and enabling the movement of labor and capital (second-degree integration) are possible via case-by-case intergovernmental agreement on those different functions of integration. Along with diplomats like Heinrich von Brentano, Walter Hallstein, and Carl Friedrich Ophüls who were more inclined to follow an institutionalist approach, it was above all Konrad Adenauer who shared it and saw in it an indispensable tool to put the Franco-German relationships into solid institutional forms (Müller-Armack 1971, pp. 69–76, 111–20).

On the way to the Treaty of Rome, a tension within the federal cabinet surfaced since Erhard opposed the institutionalist approach by summarizing its risks under "the catchword of 'harmonization'" and the tendencies toward a "bureaucratically manipulated Europe" and "supra-national dirigisme" (Erhard 1958, pp. 213–6, [1959] 1962). Müller-Armack's account of these inner-German tensions and of the negotiations with the European partners clearly indicate the significant width of integration ideas that attempted to set and shape the agenda, as well as the number of critical moments in which negotiations were at the brink of failure due to issues like the harmonization of policies, or specific sectoral privileges demanded by individual negotiating states. The fact that Walter Hallstein became the first president of the EEC Commission should certainly not be interpreted as an indication that only a decade after the end of the war, the position of the Germans was in any sense an easy one. During these years preceding the signing of the Treaty in March 1957, the cohesion between Röpke, Erhard, and Müller-Armack was still largely preserved, which was visible, for example, in their joint trip to the US in 1955 (Müller-Armack 1971, pp. 95–6). But once the Treaty was finalized and signed, Röpke and Erhard clashed (Hennecke 2005, pp. 209–16): Despite its theoretical imperfections, Erhard defended the political compromise reached in Rome and found Röpke's rhetoric in his extremely harsh public pronouncements and publications in the months after Rome, especially his address at *Aktionsgemeinschaft Soziale Marktwirtschaft* (Röpke [1957] 1958a), inappropriate. In correspondence, Erhard warned his intellectual brother in arms that the alternative would have been Erhard's abandoning the political domain and leaving the further shaping of the integration process to forces much more inimical to Röpke's ideal. He called these forces "the patent Europeans," with implicit reference to his opposition to the institutionalist ideas in Germany and beyond. Röpke accepted this reminder of the very different roles of the politician and the scholar, but nevertheless emphasized how, unlike the responsible politician, he as "the theorist without responsibility for any signature" could and should "put his weight to the other side and contribute to balancing the car in the curve" (Hennecke 2005, pp. 212–3).

Summarizing these tensions, Erhard's positions, especially during the early postwar years, were close to Röpke's and aimed at a subsidiarity-based Europe where nation-states successively transitioned to ordoliberal economic policies and respected multilateralism as embodied by GATT. And yet, Erhard increasingly understood that integration was above all a political process and required acknowledging the entangled nature of economic and political reasoning, so that only a certain degree of one's theoretical ideals could be reached within the constraints of negotiations. Such constraints included the geopolitical impasses of the opposing projects of EEC and EFTA, as well as the overarching geostrategic project of Adenauer and de Gaulle which buried Erhard's and Müller-Armack's hope that the UK-centered EFTA could merge with the EEC. Röpke suspected that, in his final decision about the essence of EEC to be a common market and not a free trade area, Erhard trusted Müller-Armack instead of Röpke. Indeed, Müller-Armack's stance was characterized by a pragmatic liberalism: He chose to be the moderate who balanced the different German positions and those of the negotiating partners

(Warneke 2013, pp. 177–90). In the final analysis, the scholar Röpke could afford to cling to his ideal of the pre-1914 order and castigate any deviations from this "first-best," while in the course of the 1950s Erhard and Müller-Armack transitioned from the principles-focused logic of academia to the compromises-focused logic of the agora, and correspondingly adopted a reasoning which often accepted the "second-best."

5.7 Conclusion: Swerving Toward a "Large Switzerland"?

The ordoliberals conducted an openly normative analysis of the potential trajectories which the European project could take that went beyond the mere identification of such trajectories (Blümle and Goldschmidt 2006). They conjectured how during its constant re-ordering in the decades to come, the project would oscillate between the visions of a "large Switzerland," that is, a politically decentralized entity which is economically integrated internally as well as non-protectionist externally, and a "large France," that is, a politically centralized entity which is economically integrated internally but protectionist externally. The explicit preference of the ordoliberals for a "large Switzerland" shaped the integration process until their leaving the public domain during the 1960s. But how about today's Europe? Can ordoliberal reasoning, as outlined in this chapter, inform politicians and especially citizens in the forthcoming years, years which will be largely dedicated to overcoming the multiple crises of the EU outlined in the introduction?

Since Jacques Delors' presidency of the European Commission (1985–1995), it is difficult to overlook a persistent movement on the "large France" trajectory, despite the lip service to the principle of subsidiary in numerous articles of the European treaties. The transformation from EEC to EU, the introduction of the euro, the increasing accumulation of competences in Brussels, and the increasing preference for bilateral trade agreements in potential conflict with the World Trade Organization's multilateralism are clear indications of this movement on the "large France" trajectory. Brexit will most probably lower the political relevance of those who favor federalism, subsidiarity, and decentralism even more. And yet, Brexit and the other crises also constitute an opportunity. As with integration in Sect. 5.3, a look at the etymology of crisis is illuminating: Among other things, *krísis* describes the situation of a crossroads where a decision about the forthcoming direction has to be taken. If Europeans switch mentally to the positive connotation of crossroads and away from the negative connotation of crash and disaster associated with a crisis, the multiple crises of our times can turn productive.

Indeed, the institutional inertia of the "large France" movement over the past 35 years is substantial, and a sudden swerve in a different direction, as required by many who employ revolutionary rhetoric vis-à-vis the EU, can easily let the European project derail. Nevertheless, if the citizen learns to appreciate the benefits of Europe à la "large Switzerland," especially if living the principle of subsidiarity becomes a widespread practice by systematically placing political processes as closely as possible to the citizen, Europe can transform over a number of years. It can regain much of the lost legitimacy, reconfigure the levels of its decision-making processes, and come closer to what has always been its crucial advantage in the eyes of European liberals: capitalizing on its diversity and harnessing decentralized decision-making as an indispensable laboratory for learning what humane combinations of liberty and order are (Feld 2012). Given the fundamental "order uncertainty" (Kolev 2020, pp. 43–4) of our age generated by the combination of globalization and digitalization, such learning in decentralized laboratories has become even more valuable than it was in the decades discussed in this chapter.

References

Berghahn, Volker R. 2015. Ordoliberalism, Ludwig Erhard, and West Germany's "Economic Basic Law". *European Review of International Studies* 2: 37–47.

Bissell, Richard M., Jr., Jonathan E. Lewis, and Frances T. Pudlo. 1996. The Marshall Plan. In *Reflections of a Cold Warrior: From Yalta to the Bay of Pigs*, ed. Richard M. Bissell Jr., Jonathan E. Lewis, and Frances T. Pudlo, 30–73. New Haven: Yale University Press.

Blümle, Gerold, and Nils Goldschmidt. 2006. From Economic Stability to Social Order: The Debate about Business Cycle Theory in the 1920s and its Relevance for the Development of Theories of Social Order by Lowe, Hayek and Eucken. *European Journal of the History of Economic Thought* 13: 543–570.

Bottici, Chiara, and Benoît Challand. 2009. Myths of Europe: A Theoretical Approach. *Journal of Educational Media, Memory & Society* 1: 9–33.

Christ, Kevin. 2018. A Measure of Judgments—Wilhelm Röpke's Methodological Heresy. *ORDO Jahrbuch für die Ordnung von Wirtschaft und Gesellschaft* 69: 35–50.

De Beers, John S. 1941. Tariff Aspects of a Federal Union. *Quarterly Journal of Economics* 56: 49–92.

Dold, Malte, and Tim Krieger, eds. 2020. *Ordoliberalism and European Economic Policy: Between Realpolitik and Economic Utopia*. London: Routledge.

Erhard, Ludwig. 1958. *Prosperity through Competition*. New York: Frederick A. Praeger.

———. [1959] 1962. Europäische Mißverständnisse. In *Deutsche Wirtschaftspolitik: Der Weg der Sozialen Marktwirtschaft*, ed. Ludwig Erhard, 450–555. Düsseldorf: Econ.

Feld, Lars P. 2012. Europa in der Welt von heute: Wilhelm Röpke und die Zukunft der Europäischen Währungsunion. *ORDO Jahrbuch für die Ordnung von Wirtschaft und Gesellschaft* 63: 403–428.

Frachebourg, Jean-Claude. 2002. HEI: une école de relations internationales pour accompagner la Société des Nations. *Le Temps Lausanne*, June 5.

Hennecke, Hans Jörg. 2005. *Wilhelm Röpke: Ein Leben in der Brandung*. Stuttgart: Schäffer-Poeschel.

Hilgerdt, Folke. 1942a. *The Network of World Trade. A Companion Volume to "Europe's Trade"*. Geneva: League of Nations.

———. 1942b. Abstract: Problems of International Economic Policy. *American Economic Review* 32: 208–209.

———. 1943. The Case for Multilateral Trade. *American Economic Review* 33: 393–407.

Jarausch, Konrad H. 2015. Economic Integration. In *Out of Ashes: A New History of Europe in the Twentieth Century*, ed. Konrad H. Jarausch, 506–532. Princeton: Princeton University Press.

Kamusella, Tomasz. 2012. Central Europe in the Distorting Mirror of Maps, Languages and Ideas. *Polish Review* 57: 33–94.

Kenney, John F. 1955. The Principle of Subsidiarity. *American Catholic Sociological Review* 16: 31–36.

Klocek di Blasio, Beata, and Bohdan Michalski. 2016. The Myth of Europe in Art and European Identities: The Divided Memory of Europe—Will Europe Succumb to Disintegration? *Politeja* 44: 101–120.

Kolev, Stefan. 2019a. Introduction: Wilhelm Röpke as a Student and Defender of Western Civilization. In *The Humane Economist: A Wilhelm Röpke Reader*, ed. Daniel J. Hugger, xv–xlii. Grand Rapids: Acton Institute.

———. 2019b. Ordoliberalism. In *Encyclopedia of Law and Economics*, ed. Alain Marciano and Giovanni Battista Ramello 1532–1537. New York: Springer.

———. 2020. F. A. Hayek, Gemeinschaft and Gesellschaft, Globalization and Digitalization. *Cosmos + Taxis Studies in Emergent Order and Organization* 7: 42–49.

Lachmann, Ludwig M. 1971. *The Legacy of Max Weber*. Berkeley: Glendessary Press.

Larres, Klaus. 1999. Torn between Idealism and Egotism: The United States and European Integration, 1945–1990. *Irish Journal of American Studies* 8: 79–118.
Machlup, Fritz. 1977. *A History of Thought on Economic Integration*. New York: Columbia University Press.
Mazower, Mark. 2008. *Hitler's Empire: How the Nazis Ruled Europe*. New York: Penguin Press.
Mueller, Wolfgang. 2009. The Soviet Union and Early West European Integration, 1947–1957: From the Brussels Treaty to the ECSC and the EEC. *Journal of European Integration History* 15: 67–85.
Müller-Armack, Alfred. 1947. *Wirtschaftslenkung und Marktwirtschaft*. Hamburg: Verlag für Wirtschaft und Sozialpolitik.
———. 1971. *Auf dem Weg nach Europa: Erinnerungen und Ausblicke*. Tübingen: Rainer Wunderlich.
Murphy, David E., Sergei A. Kondrashev, and George Bailey. 1997. The Berlin Blockade Challenges Western Ingenuity and Perseverance. In *Battleground Berlin: CIA vs. KGB in the Cold War*, ed. David E. Murphy, Sergei A. Kondrashev, and George Bailey, 51–78. New Haven: Yale University Press.
Neumann, Iver B. 1999. Making Europe: The Russian Other. In *Uses of the Other: "The East" in European Identity Formation*, ed. Iver B. Neumann, 65–112. Minneapolis: University of Minnesota Press.
Patterson, Thomas C. 1997. Civilization and Its Boosters. In *Inventing Western Civilization*, ed. Thomas C. Patterson, 27–56. New York: Monthly Review Press.
Petersen, Tim, and Michael Wohlgemuth. 2010. Wilhelm Röpke und die Europäische Integration. In *"Wort und Wirkung": Wilhelm Röpkes Bedeutung für die Gegenwart*, ed. Heinz Rieter and Joachim Zweynert, 205–243. Marburg: Metropolis.
Peukert, Helge. 1992. *Das sozialökonomische Werk Wilhelm Röpkes*. Frankfurt: Peter Lang.
Pius XI. 1931. Quadragesimo anno. *Acta Apostolicæ Sedis* 23: 177–228. Vatican City: Libreria Editrice Vaticana.
Rieter, Heinz, and Joachim Zweynert, eds. 2010. *"Wort und Wirkung": Wilhelm Röpkes Bedeutung für die Gegenwart*. Marburg: Metropolis.
Rohac, Dalibor. 2019. *In Defense of Globalism*. Lanham: Rowman & Littlefield.
Röpke, Wilhelm. 1942. *International Economic Disintegration. With an Appendix by Alexander Rüstow*. London: William Hodge.
———. [1944] 1948. *Civitas Humana: A Humane Order of Society*. London: William Hodge.
———. [1945] 1959. *International Order and Economic Integration*. Dordrecht: D. Reidel.

———. [1942] 1950. *The Social Crisis of Our Time*. Chicago: University of Chicago Press.

———. 1951. Wirtschaftssystem und internationale Ordnung: Prolegomena. *ORDO Jahrbuch für die Ordnung von Wirtschaft und Gesellschaft* 4: 261–297.

———. [1952] 1962. Deutschland als Gläubiger. In *Wirrnis und Wahrheit: Ausgewählte Aufsätze*, ed. Wilhelm Röpke, 179–182. Erlenbach-Zurich: Eugen Rentsch.

———. 1954. Wege zur Konvertibilität. In *Die Konvertibilität der europäischen Währungen*, ed. Albert Hunold, 76–122. Erlenbach-Zurich: Eugen Rentsch.

———. 1955. *Europäische Wirtschaftsintegration—gestern und heute*. Duisburg: Schriften der Volks- und Betriebswirtschaftlichen Vereinigung im rheinisch-westfälischen Industriegebiet.

———. 1957. Europa als wirtschaftliche Aufgabe. In *Europa—Besinnung und Hoffnung*, ed. Albert Hunold, 159–184. Erlenbach-Zurich: Eugen Rentsch.

———. [1957] 1958a. Gemeinsamer Markt und Freihandelszone. In *Welche Wirtschaftspolitik kann das Vertrauen des Wählers rechtfertigen?*, ed. Aktionsgemeinschaft Soziale Marktwirtschaft, 18–32. Ludwigsburg: Martin Hoch.

———. 1958b. Gemeinsamer Markt und Freihandelszone: 28 Thesen als Richtpunkte. *ORDO Jahrbuch für die Ordnung von Wirtschaft und Gesellschaft* 10: 31–62.

———. 1959. Zwischenbilanz der europäischen Wirtschaftsintegration: Kritische Nachlese. *ORDO Jahrbuch für die Ordnung von Wirtschaft und Gesellschaft* 11: 69–94.

———. [1958] 2009. Europa—Einheit in der Vielfalt. In *Marktwirtschaft ist nicht genug: Gesammelte Aufsätze*, ed. Hans Jörg Hennecke, 235–249. Waltrop: Manuscriptum.

———. [1942] 2015. A Value Judgment on Value Judgments. *Journal of Markets & Morality* 18: 497–514.

Rosenberg, Hans. 1943. Sowjetische Luftpolitik gegen Europa. *Zeitschrift für Politik* 33: 344–350.

Russell, I. Willis. 1944. Among the New Words. *American Speech* 19: 222–226.

Sally, Razeen. 1994. The Social Market and Liberal Order: Theory and Policy Implications. *Government and Opposition* 29: 461–476.

———. 1999. Wilhelm Röpke and International Economic Order: 'Liberalism from Below'. *ORDO Jahrbuch für die Ordnung von Wirtschaft und Gesellschaft* 50: 47–51.

Salter, Mark B. 2002. Civilization and Barbarians. In *Barbarians and Civilization in International Relations*, ed. Mark B. Salter, 8–27. London: Pluto Press.

Schüller, Richard. 1950. Economic Integration of Western Europe. *Social Research* 17: 320–331.

Siebert, Horst. 2005. *The German Economy: Beyond the Social Market*. Princeton: Princeton University Press.

Slobodian, Quinn. 2018. *Globalists: The End of Empire and the Birth of Neoliberalism*. Cambridge: Harvard University Press.

Spawforth, A.J., and Susan Walker. 1985. The World of the Panhellenion. I. Athens and Eleusis. *Journal of Roman Studies* 75: 78–104.

Thode, Stefan. 2003. *Integration in unternehmensinternen sozialen Beziehungen*. Wiesbaden: Deutscher Universitäts-Verlag.

Warneke, Sara. 2013. *Die europäische Wirtschaftsintegration aus der Perspektive Wilhelm Röpkes*. Stuttgart: Lucius & Lucius.

Wegner, Gerhard. 2020a. Ordoliberalism and Democracy: How the Interwar Period Changed the Agenda of German Liberalism. In *Ordoliberalism and European Economic Policy: Between Realpolitik and Economic Utopia*, ed. Malte Dold and Tim Krieger, 39–57. London: Routledge.

———. 2020b. Reassessing the Dependence of Capitalism on Democracy—The Case of Imperial Germany and the Weimar Republic. *Journal of Institutional Economics* 16: 337–354.

Zweig, Stefan. [1942] 1943. *The World of Yesterday: An Autobiography*. London: Cassell & Co.

CHAPTER 6

Hayek's Europe: The Austrian School and European Federalism

Dalibor Rohac and Alberto Mingardi

6.1 Introduction

Although the efforts of modern classical liberals revolve primarily around an intellectual agenda for the domestic reform of institutions and policies leading to a reduction in the size, scope, and discretionary powers of the state, it is impossible to dissociate them from questions of the international economic order. The connection between the two was particularly vivid to the founding generation of the Mont Pelerin Society (MPS), an association that reunited liberal scholars and reinvigorated the intellectual movement, which then enjoyed the heyday of its influence during the

D. Rohac (✉)
American Enterprise Institute, Washington, DC, USA

Wilfried Martens Centre for European Studies, Brussels, Belgium
e-mail: Dalibor.Rohac@aei.org

A. Mingardi
IULM University, Milan, Italy

Bruno Leoni Institute, Milan, Italy
e-mail: alberto.mingardi@brunoleoni.it; alberto.mingardi@iulm.it

F. Giavazzi et al. (eds.), *The Liberal Heart of Europe*,
https://doi.org/10.1007/978-3-030-60368-7_6

Thatcher and Reagan years. Among MPS' founding figures, a number of prominent thinkers were vocal proponents of international federalism: a program that would simultaneously push for the decentralization of states, while embedding them within a supranational framework that would curb their capacity to wage war and engage in protectionist and mercantilist policies.

When the Walter Lippmann Colloquium, a precursor to the Mont Pelerin Society, convened in Paris in August 1938, the most pressing items on the agenda included countering the excesses of nationalism, militarism, and the rise of totalitarian ideologies, which were dragging Europe into war. The agenda of the meeting thus included sessions on the "co-existence of liberal and totalitarian economies," "economic and psychologic policy of liberal states toward totalitarian ones," "economics of war," "economic policy of liberal states between themselves," and other pressing questions of international political economy (Hartwell 1995, p. 21). The attendees included the polymath Michael Polanyi (1891–1976), Austrian economists Ludwig von Mises (1881–1973) and Friedrich von Hayek (1899–1992), and Jacques Rueff (1896–1978), the future advisor to President de Gaulle, as well as Wilhelm Röpke (1899–1966) and Walter Eucken (1891–1950), the doyens of German "Ordo-liberalism," the group of scholars that paved the way for the German "economic miracle."

The founding meeting of the Mont Pelerin Society in April 1947, which also included key figures of classical liberal thought in America, such as Milton Friedman (1912–2006), Aaron Director (1901–2004), and Frank Knight (1885–1972), featured sessions on "The Future of Germany" (Röpke opened the discussion) and "Problems and Chances of European Federation"—the discussion was opened by Bertrand de Jouvenel (1903–1987). The meeting, which already revealed significant fault lines within liberal thought—including on questions of social and cultural conservatism and the proper role of government within the economy—took place at a time when the contours of the postwar international order were still uncertain. Communist parties, heavily supported by Stalin, were on the rise in Western Europe, the Marshall Plan was still months away, and the prospects of another conflict or a Soviet takeover of the continent were far from hysterical.

Not only were classical liberals of the time preoccupied by questions of international order, many shared a common outlook of how international affairs ought to be organized among free societies. Instead of unfettered sovereignty for nation-states, a rules-based system transcending national boundaries needed to be devised to curb the destructive and protectionist capabilities of nation-states.

This chapter explores, through the writings of Friedrich Hayek, Luigi Einaudi (1874–1961), and Ludwig von Mises, the reasons that led classical liberals to converge on the idea of international federalism and the goals that such federation would accomplish, as well as the practical attributes of its functioning. The choice of these three classical liberal thinkers is not accidental. In spite of different career trajectories and political sensibilities, the three shared the lived experience of a European continent tormented by the demons of nationalism, witnessing the undoing of the extraordinary achievements of the "first age of globalization," which was brought to an end in 1914.

Hayek moved from Vienna to London in the early 1930s, well before the *Anschluss*. He was a member of the Federal Union, the British federalist association created in 1938 which set up the Federal Union Research Institute, where classical liberal ideas on federalism were at least briefly discussed (Rosenboim 2014; Milani 2016). The context was one in which, with Europe once more becoming a theater of war, it became clear that what happened in Versailles at the end of WWI was "a misunderstanding": "Liberal Englishmen and Americans … were saying, People who are self-governing are likely to be governed well, therefore we are in favor of self-determination; whereas their interlocutors were saying People who live in their own national states are the only free people, therefore we claim self-determination" (Kedourie [1960] 1985, p. 133).

Self-determination, which was supposed to free European people from unjust government, led to even more national conflicts in the German-speaking world and, ultimately, to WWII.

Einaudi, nowadays best known as the first president of Italy (1948–1955), wrote extensively on international matters. Because of his political role and also of his influence on Ernesto Rossi (1897–1967), one of the authors of the Ventotene manifesto *For a Free and United Europe*, Einaudi is sometimes acknowledged as a founding father of the European Union (EU). An applied economist by training, he was for his entire life a vocal participant in the public debate. He began writing for newspapers in his youth and took part in the public debate for his whole adult life. His personal prestige was such that, in 1946, after the fall of Fascism and Italy's liberation from Nazi occupation, he became in rapid succession Governor of the Central Bank, Treasury Minister, and Head of State. One of the hallmarks of postwar Italy was the rejection of protectionism, which

Fascism had pursued under the name of "autarky," for a full-fledged commitment to European integration, with Einaudi as perhaps its most vocal advocate.

The case of Ludwig von Mises is also telling. A product of Viennese intellectual ferment of the early years of the twentieth century, Mises never experienced the same degree of academic recognition as Hayek, who went on to receive a Nobel Prize in economics. But Mises inspired Hayek's work and was at the forefront of the so-called economic calculation debate in the 1920s and 1930s, which focused on the feasibility of a centrally planned economy.

Both Hayek and Mises have become, however, iconic for slightly different strands of the classical liberal movement: Hayek more palatable to a broader audience within the social sciences and more engaged with research across social sciences, Mises more intransigent, more consistent in the eyes of his admirers, nothing but a doctrinaire to his critics and opponents. By the time Mises left Austria for Switzerland and later, under dramatic wartime circumstances, for the United States, he already had a history of working for the leading voice of the Paneuropean Movement, the Count of Coudenhove-Kalergi (1894–1972). Just like in Hayek's and Einaudi's case, it was the wartime period that led him to articulate his views of international federalism more fully.

All three rejected the notion that socialism and nationalism were polar opposites or "that National Socialism was not socialism, just something contemptible" (Hayek 1994, p. 102). In practice, as witnessed by the three throughout the interwar period, nationalism and socialism went hand in hand. Their embrace of European federalism was a response to that experience.

6.2 Why a Federation?

There were several, mutually connected objectives that these classical liberals were hoping that an international federation in Europe would accomplish, all of them connected to Hayek's realization that "one of the main deficiencies of nineteenth-century liberalism was that its advocates did not sufficiently realize that the achievement of the recognized harmony of interests between the inhabitants of the different states was only possible within the framework of international security" (Hayek [1939] 1948, p. 270). These were not abstract concerns, but rather they involved the very pressing question of how the conflicts of the first half of the twentieth century and the rise of totalitarian ideologies could be stopped. Hayek's response was that maintaining and deepening the economic interdependence of European societies not only was conducive to economic prosperity but also reduced the risk of nationalist, *beggar-thy-neighbor* policies and of conflict. Sustaining such an economic policy regime, in turn, involved restraining the power of nation-states by setting up a dedicated supranational authority.

The first and most pressing of the aims of liberal "international federalists" involved the sheer survival of free societies, especially the smaller geopolitically vulnerable ones. This arose with urgency as the war in Europe was ending and it was becoming obvious that Stalin's ambition was the incorporation of the entire Eurasian landmass into a Soviet-dominated political order. In his first book published after his arrival in the United States, *Omnipotent Government*, Ludwig von Mises (1944) argued that "if the Western democracies do not succeed in establishing a permanent union, the fruits of victory will be lost again." For the small citizenries of Europe in particular, such as the Dutch, the Danes, or the Norwegians, "the alternative to incorporation into a new democratic supernational system is not unrestricted sovereignty but ultimate subjugation by the totalitarian power" (Mises 1944, pp. 255–56). In 1919, Mises had warned of the consequences of the punitive terms of the Treaty of Versailles (Mises [1919] 2006).

Secondly, the end of the war brought about a reckoning with the cultural and moral fallout of Germany's descent into tyranny and barbarism in the 1930s. The horrors of Nazism were such that Hayek, alongside others, harbored doubts about the prospects of Europe as a continent of civilized nations. In his talk to the Political Society at King's College, Cambridge University, he stated:

> Whether we shall be able to rebuild something like a common European civilisation after this war will be decided mainly by what happens in the years immediately following it. It is possible that the events that will accompany the collapse of Germany will cause such destruction as to remove the whole of Central Europe for generations or perhaps permanently from the orbit of European civilisation. It seems unlikely that, if this happens, the developments can be confined to Central Europe; and if the fate of Europe should be to relapse into barbarism, though ultimately a new civilisation may emerge from it, it is not likely that this country would escape the consequences. The future of England is tied up with the future of Europe, and,

> whether we like it or not, the future of Europe will largely be decided by what will happen in Germany. Our efforts at least must be directed towards regaining Germany for those values on which European civilisation was built and which alone can form the basis from which we can move towards the realisation of the ideals which guide us. (Hayek [1944] 1992, p. 201)

What was to blame for Germany's experiment with barbarism was not simply the political dynamics of the interwar period and the appeal of Nazi ideology. Hayek was inclined to agree with Röpke that National Socialism was an extension of the much earlier project of Germany's political consolidation and militarization—and therefore that "the victors should not regard Bismarck's creation of a highly centralised Germany as an irreversible fact, and that, if Germany is ever to fit as a peaceful member into the European family of nations, it will be necessary partly to undo Bismarck's work and to reconstruct Germany with a decentralised and truly federal structure" (Hayek [1945] 1946, p. 12).

International federalism was a holistic project as it involved not just binding European nations into a larger political unit but also decentralizing them, especially Germany, for whom Hayek envisaged a gradual restoration of its political self-governance in exchange as it succeeds in building democratic federal institutions "retaining in the end no more control over the individual state than corresponds to the minimum power of a federal government" (Hayek [1945] 1946, p. 13). To succeed, this policy of domestic decentralization had to "be supplement[ed] by the enforcement of complete free trade, external and internal, for all these German states" (Hayek [1945] 1946, p. 13). Indeed, Einaudi also maintained that the idea of a federation was in itself "the opposite of subjugating the various states and the various regions to a single centre" (Einaudi 1945a).

The third aim of international federalism, to ensure the existence of a regime of free trade, was directly related to the overarching objective of securing peace. Peace requires a free economy and trade as well as an effective international order of law and the abolition of national sovereignty. Whatever scheme for political interstate union, Hayek admonishes, "would not last long unless accompanied by economic union" (Hayek [1939] 1948, p. 258). Thus, an interstate federation should "do away with the impediments as to the movement of men, goods, and capital between the states and render possible the creation of common rules of law, a uniform monetary system, and common control of communications" (Hayek [1939] 1948, p. 255). Economic union is important because it extends the order of market-based cooperation across national borders, creating material incentives for peaceful coexistence. In contrast, when left to their own devices, nation-states are conflict-prone since "all conflicts of interests tend to become conflicts between the same groups of people, instead of conflicts between groups of constantly varying composition. The peoples are projected in conflicts between states, which hide the reality that the interests of inhabitants are not always the interests of the nation" (p. 257). Of course, for Hayek, "one of the virtues of a market system is that it allows people with very different values to express their desires through the market" (Caldwell 2003, p. 239), whereas one of the vices of nation-states is that they transform differences in values into occasions for conflict.

While the classical liberal tradition of international federalism emphasized the need for imposing external constraints on the power of nation-states, some of its proponents went further and rejected, like Einaudi, the entire idea "of the sovereign state, of the state which, within its territorial limits, can make laws regardless of what happens outside those limits" as "an idol of the formalistic legal mind and does not match any reality." Furthermore, Einaudi argues, the concept is ultimately incompatible with a life in a modern, commercial society:

> A thousand and a thousand bonds tie men of a given nation to men of every other state. The claim to absolute sovereignty cannot be carried out within the limits of the so-called sovereign state. Men, in modern life dominated by the division of labour, by the great mechanised workshops, by rapid international communications, by the tendency to a high standard of living, cannot live, if their life is reduced to the limits of the state. (Einaudi 1945b)

Building on Smith's insight that "the division of labour is limited by the extent of the market," Einaudi saw the modern nation-state as basically *anachronistic* in the face of a highly internationally integrated, market economy. Given their sizes, "the modern European states are—economically—pygmies. Their surface is too small for a genuine division of labour to establish within their borders" (Einaudi [1952] 1956). Other classical liberals might not have rejected the nation-state out of hand, but they understood the need for internationally integrated markets, hence the need for the European federation.

Both Hayek and Mises argued that the absence of tariffs and free movement of people and capital will "limit to a great extent the scope of the economic policy of the individual states." The Union will become "a one single market" and "prices in its different parts will differ only by the costs of transport" (Hayek [1939] 1948, pp. 258–59). Any change in the condition of production in one country will reverberate elsewhere. This means, for Hayek, that government interventions aiming at interfering with the price system and subsidizing production with "monopolistic organisation of individual industries" will soon cease to be at the disposal of governments (p. 259). They will certainly be able to support particular groups of producers, but "they will have to do so by direct subsidies from funds raised by ordinary taxation" (p. 259), instead of limiting consumers' choices through tariffs or other forms of protectionism. However, because differences in economic policy and interventions enacted by countries create trade frictions, a genuinely integrated European (or global) economy thus requires either a shared regime of generalized laissez-faire or delegating the power to regulate and intervene in the economy to the supernational authority, Mises notes: "If a country does not want to abandon government interference with business, and nevertheless renounces protectionism in its relations with the other member nations of the new union to be formed, it must vest all power in the authority ruling this union and *completely* surrender its own sovereignty to the supernational authority" (Mises 1944, p. 267).

Hayek offers an elegant solution to this dilemma by suggesting that efforts at centrally organized economic intervention would be self-limiting in a heterogeneous union in which the concentration of benefits and costs would be more obvious than in more cohesive political units, in which favors to special interests are often masqueraded as being in the "national interest." With great diversity of nationalities and interests and only a weak sense of community and pan-European pride, it becomes much more difficult to sell the clamoring of particular pressure groups as the expression of general or national interest. "Is it likely that the French peasant will be willing to pay more for his fertilizer to help the British chemical industry? Will the Swedish workman be ready to pay more for his oranges to assist the Californian grower?" (Hayek [1939] 1948, p. 262).

The absence of national cohesion and a shared public square in an entity like the European Union in Hayek's view imposes as a constraint on interventionism policies of governments. The absence of national cohesion would similarly limit the expansion of the welfare state and other forms of social protection: "even such legislation as the limitation of working hours or compulsory unemployment insurance, or the protection of amenities, will be viewed in a different light in poor and in rich regions and may in the former actually harm and rouse violent opposition from the kind of people who in the richer regions demand it and profit from it" (Hayek [1939] 1948, p. 263).

6.3 Architecture of a European Federation

The classical liberals' arguments for an international federation are often presented in a somewhat abstract fashion—and certainly not a concrete agenda of institutional reform, with Röpke's extensive commentary on the process of European integration as it unfolded in the 1950s being a notable exception (see Kolev's contribution to 2020, Chap. 5). The question of how the federation ought to be organized politically, how powers ought to be divided between branches, and what checks and balances should be instituted remains largely orthogonal to the classical liberal project. However, it is safe to say that classical liberals did not seek to recreate the nation-state on a larger scale. Instead they scrupulously insisted on applying the principle of subsidiarity in institutional design. Mises cites Switzerland and the (early) United States as examples of successful federations, in which the powers of the central government were tightly limited: "To the federal government those matters were assigned which went beyond the boundaries of the states: foreign affairs, defense against foreign aggression, the safeguarding of trade between the states, the management of the postal service and of customs" (Mises 1944, p. 267).

Likewise, a European federation should thus be vested only with powers *subsidiary* to those held by lower levels of government, which cannot be adequately exercised by nation-states or local governments. Accordingly, Hayek says,

> planning in a federation cannot assume the forms which today are pre-eminently known under this term; that there must be no substitution of day-to-day interference and regulation for the impersonal forces of the market ... In a federation economic policy will have to take the form of providing a rational permanent framework within which individual initiative will have the largest possible scope and will be made to work as beneficently as possible; and it will have to supplement the working of the competitive mechanism where, in the nature of the case, certain services cannot be brought forth and be regulated by the price system. (Hayek [1939] 1948, pp. 268–69)

Similarly, for Einaudi, federalism "from an economic point of view means assigning to the federal authority certain economic tasks strictly defined in the constitutional document of the federation ... it is necessary to reduce to a minimum absolutely necessary the number of tasks assigned to the federation from the beginning" (Einaudi 1945a). Such tasks include the regulation of transport, commerce with foreign states, and the freeing up of trade within the boundaries of the federation. They thus aim basically at reducing transaction costs: for this reason, he also foresaw a common currency. It is worth remembering that he also thought that "the abolition of the sovereignty of individual states in monetary matters" is good in itself.

> Whoever remembers the bad use that many states had made and make the right to coin money cannot doubt the urgency of removing them from such a right. It was essentially reduced to the right to falsify the currency ... The devaluation of the Italian lira and the Deutsche Mark, which ruined the middle classes and fed the malaise of workers, produced the gangs of unemployed intellectuals and troublemakers who gave power to dictators. If the European federation takes away from the individual federated states the possibility of coping with public works by making the ticket press groan, and will force them to provide for them only with taxes and voluntary loans, it will have, for this only, accomplished something great. (Einaudi 1945a)

Hayek too takes it as a given that a federation would have to use a common monetary unit. Perhaps, a system of fixed exchange rates could be introduced, similar to the gold standard. Presciently, he notes, that

> It appears doubtful whether, in a Union with a universal monetary system, independent national central banks would continue to exist; they would probably have to be organized into a sort of Federal Reserve System. But, in any case, a national monetary policy which was predominantly guided by the economic and financial conditions of the individual state would inevitably lead to the disruption of the universal monetary system. (Hayek [1939] 1948, p. 259)

In any event, the thrust of the federation's powers ought to be negative, "preventing individual states from interfering with economic activity in certain ways" without necessarily holding also the "positive power of acting in their stead" (Hayek [1939] 1948, p. 267). Still, Hayek and Mises were under no illusions about the tension that existed between their vision of international federalism and the reality of government involvement in the economy as it existed in their time.

Hayek's hopeful prediction that federal-level interventionism would be self-limiting was based on the presence of incentives against economic interventionism, resulting from the internal diversity of the federation. Mises, however, saw those as "not unsurmountable" (Mises 1944, p. 268) and pointed to the experiences of Switzerland and the United States, where the combination of widespread economic interventionism and absent interstate trade barriers "[shifted] the political center of gravity to the federal government. Seen from the formalistic viewpoint of constitutional law, the United States and the Swiss Confederation may doubtless still be classified as federations, but in actual fact they are moving more and more toward centralization" (Mises 1944, p. 268).

6.4 Has the EU Been a Classical Liberal Project?

Contemporary Euroskepticism on the political right shares a lot with Mises' prediction that the "international body for foreign trade planning would be an assembly of the delegates of governments attached to the ideas of hyper-protectionism" (Mises 1944, p. 250). While the European project, as it evolved since the 1950s, was definitely a classical liberal enterprise, but one that reflected a variety of interests and ideological outlooks, there have been aspects of the European integration process that do confirm Hayek's prediction "that the integration of previously sovereign nation-states in Europe would reduce the capacity of states to regulate the capitalist economy and to burden it with the costs of an expensive welfare state" (Scharpf 2010, p. 239).

The liberalizing role of the European project has to do in large part with the role played by the European Court of Justice in upholding the precedents created by cases such as *Dassonville*, which effectively prohibited countries from using regulations that have the same effects as traditional forms of protectionism. "All trading rules," the Court decided, "enacted by Member States, which are capable of hindering, directly or indirectly, actually or potentially, intra-Community trade are to be considered as measures having an effect equivalent to quantitative restrictions" (European Court of Justice 1974). Likewise, in the *Cassis de Dijon* case (European Court of Justice 1979), the Court effectively laid down mutual recognition of standards of safety, health, environment, and consumer protection among countries of the European Economic Community as the basic operating principle of the single market. The Single European Act was a highly complicated piece of legislation, with consequences that went far beyond just economic integration (e.g. covering questions of voting procedures, the European Commission's powers in areas of environmental, social, and regional policy), yet at its heart its purpose was to assure the free movement of goods, people, services, and capital (Gillingham 2003, pp. 228–58). The 1980s and the 1990s also saw the rise of the European Commission's role as an authority on competition policy. From a classical liberal perspective, its scrutiny of mergers between large private actors might be seen as objectionable, its role in curbing state aid to national champions and breaking up publicly owned monopolies in network industries has been an unmitigated success—likewise has its role in deregulating the airline industry and dismantling barriers to the integration of financial markets across Europe. State aid rules are a unique feature of the EU legal framework. With a few exceptions, they ban any discretionary intervention from member states that may result in a distortion of the commerce between or within the member states themselves. The relative rigidity in their enforcement in the past few decades has been a primary ingredient in the attempt to create a level playing field across European firms. As a result of the EU's commitment to the single market, a number of product and service markets in Europe, most prominently airlines and telecom, seem more competitive today than in the United States (Gutiérrez and Philippon 2019).

It is of course true that the operation of the single market is shaped by bargains struck between national governments, which have not abandoned their penchant for economic interventionism, as well as by the regulatory activism of the European authorities (Reho 2016, pp. 32–40). That does not detract from the fact that the single market is the closest example to a genuinely integrated economy one can find outside of actual unitary states. Furthermore, it would be a significant error to disregard the role of the European project in meeting two of the original aims of international federalism: preventing the continent from becoming captured by totalitarian powers and bringing Germany back into the community of civilized nations. In both of those instances, economic integration went in tandem with the defense umbrella provided to the continent by the United States, while effectively disarming Western Europe for the duration of the Cold War. However, the complementarity between a common framework of security and economic integration was obvious to the founding generation of the contemporary classical liberal movement. However much the

European project might fall short of classical liberal prescriptions, it is worth remembering Mises' stark articulation of the problem the federation was meant to address: "Let us not forget that such a union must be established if any peace scheme is to work. The alternative to the realization of a union of the Western democracies is a return to the ominous conditions prevailing from 1918 to 1939, and consequently to new and still more dreadful wars" (Mises 1944, p. 271).

References

Caldwell, Bruce. 2003. *Hayek's Challenge: An Intellectual Biography of F.A. Hayek*. Chicago: The University of Chicago Press.

Einaudi, Luigi. 1945a. *I problemi economici della federazione europea*. Milan: Edizioni La Fiaccola. Accessed June 29, 2020. http://www.luigieinaudi.it/doc/i-problemi-economici-della-federazione-europea-2/?id=282.

———. 1945b. Il mito dello Stato sovrano. *Il Risorgimento Liberale*, January 3. Accessed June 29, 2020. http://www.luigieinaudi.it/doc/il-mito-dello-stato-sovrano/?id=531.

———, ed. (1952) 1956. Tipi e connotati della federazione discorrendo di comunità europea di difesa. In *Lo scrittoio del Presidente (1948–1955)*, 62–84. Turin: Einaudi Editore.

European Court of Justice. 1974. *Procureur du Roi v Benoît and Gustave Dassonville*. Case 8/74, July 11. Accessed June 29, 2020. http://eur-lex.europa.eu/legal-content/EN/TXT/?uri=CELEX:61974CJ0008.

———. 1979. *Rewe-Zentral AG v Bundesmonopolverwaltung für Branntwein*. Case 120/78, February 20. Accessed June 29, 2020. http://eur-lex.europa.eu/legal-content/EN/TXT/?uri=CELEX%3A61978CJ0120.

Gillingham, John. 2003. *European Integration 1950–2003: Superstate or New Market Economy?* Cambridge: Cambridge University Press.

Gutiérrez, Germán, and Thomas Philippon. 2019. How EU Markets Became More Competitive Than US Markets: A Study of Institutional Drift. NBER Working Paper 24700. Cambridge, MA: National Bureau of Economic Research.

Hartwell, Ronald M. 1995. *A History of the Mont Pelerin Society*. Indianapolis, Indiana: Liberty Fund.

von Hayek, Frederick A. (1945) 1946. Introduction. In *The German Question*, ed. Wilhelm Röpke and trans. E.W. Dickes, 11–14. London: George Allen & Unwin.

———. (1939) 1948. The Economic Conditions of Interstate Federalism. *New Commonwealth Quarterly* 5: 131–149. Now in *Individualism and Economic Order*, 255–272. Chicago: University of Chicago Press.

———. (1944) 1992. Historians and the Future of Europe. Talk Delivered at King's College Cambridge, February 28. *R. M. Hartwell Papers 4/0*, Hoover

Institution Archives. In *The Fortunes of Liberalism: Essays on Austrian Economics and the Ideal of Freedom*, ed. Peter G. Klein, 201–15. Indianapolis, Indiana: Liberty Fund.
———. 1994. *Hayek on Hayek: An Autobiographical Dialogue*. Edited by Stephen Kresge and Leif Wenar. Chicago: The University of Chicago Press.
Kedourie, Elie. (1960) 1985. *Nationalism*. London: Hutchinson.
Kolev, Stefan. 2020. 'Large Switzerland' or 'Large France'? The Ordoliberal and Early European Integration. In *The Liberal Heart of Europe: Essays in Memory of Alberto Giovannini*, ed. Francesco Giavazzi, Francesco Lefebvre D'Ovidio, and Alberto Mingardi, Chapter 5. London: Palgrave Macmillan.
Milani, Tommaso. 2016. From Laissez-Faire to Supranational Planning: The Economic Debate Within Federal Union (1938–1945). *European Review of History: Revue européenne d'histoire* 23: 664–685.
von Mises, Ludwig. 1944. *Omnipotent Government: The Rise of the Total State and Total War*. New Haven, CT: Yale University Press.
———. (1919) 2006. *Nation, State, and Economy: Contributions to the Politics and History of Our Time*. Edited by Bettina B. Greaves and translated by Leland B. Yeager. Indianapolis, Indiana: Liberty Fund.
Reho, Federico O., ed. 2016. Federalismo hayekiano e integrazione Europea. In *Le condizioni economiche del federalismo fra Stati*, ed. Friedrich A. von Hayek. Soveria Mannelli, Italy: Rubbettino.
Rosenboim, O.R. 2014. Barbara Wootton, Friedrich Hayek and the Debate on Democratic Federalism in the 1940s. *The International History Review* 36: 894–918.
Scharpf, Fritz W. 2010. The Asymmetry of European Integration, or Why the EU Cannot Be a 'Social Market Economy. *Socio-Economic Review* 8: 211–250.

CHAPTER 7

The Monnet Method and the Obsolescence of the EU

John R. Gillingham III

Might one be permitted—at least by way of introduction—to ask *not* how "academic scribblers end up enslaving practical men" but rather how "practical men enslave academic scribblers." The founders of the two institutions that eventuated in the European Union (EU)—the European Coal and Steel Community (ECSC) of 1952 and the European Economic Community (EEC) of 1958—were senior civil servants and diplomats rather than intellectuals or economists and the motivation behind their work had less to do with any particular theory than with shared experience, above all that of the still recent world war. Grand ideas hardly entered into the picture—be they those of a Keynes, a Hayek, or a Röpke. Further, no overarching intellectual rationale has shaped the subsequent history of the EU, which is one of fits and starts resulting from the interplay of exogenous circumstances and the weird dynamics of a self-serving bureaucracy.

One still wonders whether the origins of the EU should be traced back to the founding of the ECSC or that of the EEC. The latter grew out only

J. R. Gillingham III (✉)
University of Missouri–St. Louis, St. Louis, MO, USA
e-mail: gillinghamj@umsl.edu

F. Giavazzi et al. (eds.), *The Liberal Heart of Europe*,
https://doi.org/10.1007/978-3-030-60368-7_7

in part from the former. Although memories of WWII were uppermost in the concerns of the men who organized both institutions, their motivations differed, as did the character of the institutions that emerged from their respective sets of negotiations. The fit between the two somewhat different traditions—the former basically statist in inspiration and the latter mainly market-oriented—has always been less than perfect.

The inception of "European integration," as the term is customarily understood, will forever be associated with the extraordinary personage of Jean Monnet. Monnet was the author of the famous 1950 Schuman Plan and the architect of the institution based upon it, the ECSC. He was no theorist but something *sui generis*, a brilliant international political operative driven by a single-minded pursuit of his vision, European unification. He would also inspire a bureaucratic cult that survived him. Although much ink has been spilled in discussion of the supposed "Monnet Method," there was in truth no single such thing, unless it was to work behind the scenes through well-placed policy-makers loyal to him personally. He had little use for democracy other than to provide a veneer of legitimacy for institutions of his design.

Monnet was a senior government official with the unique distinction of having worked on behalf of France, Great Britain, and the United States in each of the two great armed struggles of the last century. Perhaps no single individual could claim more experience as a manager of war economies. He was in fact the indispensable statesman of the post-WWII years, the only person both with a design for the future and in a position to implement it.

Monnet's immense reputation went long unchallenged but now must be examined critically. His grand projects, though well-intentioned, in fact posed both short- and long-term threats to representative government and economic growth. Moreover, his lasting legacy was a rigid mindset—an institutionalized and pervasive pattern of thinking about the phenomenon of European integration—that has ossified over time and obstructs discussion not only of alternatives to the present EU (and EMU) but of ways to reform it. The EU/EMU is thus becoming an anachronism whose malfunctioning is wreaking damage on the causes it purports to serve, and whose days are almost assuredly numbered.

Obsessed, in 1950, with the question of French security rather than the economics of heavy industry, Monnet designed the European Coal and Steel Community as a narrowly conceived sectoral institution for the public regulation of only a single branch of production, the traditionally cartelized heavy industry of Western Europe. This required restricting competition rather than promoting it. Although in the event the ECSC was a diplomatic and public relations triumph, it was no less an economic failure. The mines never pulled out of their long-term decline, and the new foundries of Europe would be built along coastlines instead of inland regions like the Ruhr in order to access cheap overseas sources of combustible. The dreaded German *Verbundwirtschaft* (the tied-in, trustified economy whose English vernacular is simply "The Ruhr") turned out to be a bogeyman—an artifact of the past, a victim of economic and technological change. Economically and strategically, the importance of coal and steel would, furthermore, rapidly decline in the nuclear age.

The unraveling and dissolution of the ECSC in the late 1950s did not frustrate Monnet's vaulting ambitions, as manifest spectacularly in his dramatic proposal, which failed in 1954, for a European Defense Community (EDC) organized around a full-scale new Euro-army of nationally integrated units; this was an initiative far more sweeping than anything since brought to bear in European high politics. His scheme also included provisions that would have resulted in a European version of the military-industrial complex then forming in the United States. Monnet even drafted plans for a future European *Political* Community which, if ever realized, would have more closely resembled neo-authoritarian governments like Putin's Russia than the parliamentary democracies that still exist in the West.

With the EDC debacle alive in memory, Monnet was excluded from a new round of European negotiations of the so-called six signatories of the Treaty of Rome, which led to the formation of the EEC in 1958 and the eventual EU. He influenced these talks chiefly through the French delegation. The overarching purpose of the Messina negotiators was, of course, to construct an institution that could prevent the recurrence of the terrible warfare that threatened the survival of European civilization. This required applying the lessons of the American war economy to European reconstruction. An obvious one was that sheer size—bigness—was critical to the recent war's outcome. Called for was political and economic reorganization on a continental scale, which presupposed both political reconciliation between France and Germany and the creation of markets broad and deep enough to capture the economic benefits of the new war-winning production methods and breakthrough technologies.

The immediate aim of the Messina parties from Italy, Germany, and the Benelux nations was modest, sensible, and forward-looking: to create a single customs area and a Common Market that would reinstate Germany as the economic motor of Europe's economic growth. To clinch the necessary deal, however, they had to give way to the other party, France. The result was a patchwork founding treaty in the form of a liberal framework agreement which, for better or worse, left different developmental paths open.

The Treaty of Rome included various awkward concessions to the French, some of eventual importance, others of little significance. One of them enshrined a special role for France in Africa (Eurafrica). Another was the creation of Monnet's questionable special project for Euratom, an independent executive authority conceived as a rough counterpart to the American Atomic Energy Commission, which, however, unlike the US agency but in line with his strategic priorities, combined statutory military as well as civilian functions. Neither of these ideas had much traction in the eventual politics of integration.

The story was different with regard to a third demand of the French negotiating team, a price-support scheme for farmers. Like the ECSC a protectionist scheme, what emerged from the talks became the Common Agricultural Policy (CAP), which henceforth would become by far the largest item in the EU budget and, as a powerful lobby, the most important source of the organization's political strength. It still poses the major impediment to trans-Atlantic free trade.

It also set an important precedent. The only other noteworthy project of the first twenty years of the EU's history was the Davignon Plan, an ambitious *dirigiste* modernization scheme for eliminating excess capacity in the European steel industry by means of a public super-cartel. As a result of it, the minimill revolution, which transformed much of the American steel industry, would bypass Europe. The Davignon price-support Plan should share the blame with the American steel dinosaurs for creating a bitter legacy issue in US-EU economic diplomacy.

Such EU programs as these, and many others like them, both realized and abortive, were characteristic of decades in which, regardless of the specific term one uses—be it organized capitalism, industrial policy, *planisme*, or whatever—corporatism reigned in economic policy-making at both the national and European levels and on both sides of the Atlantic. Now, many years later, it seems to be enjoying a desperate revival.

For the first two decades of its existence, the EEC remained largely a paper project. It contributed little to the economic growth of the 1950s and 1960s, but thanks to the emotional appeal of the European Idea could count on the blessings of an uninformed public. Such a "permissive consensus" would disappear once the EU became a serious player in European politics. This happened after the ambitious "re-relaunch" initiated by the neo-Monnetist, Jacques Delors, in the mid-1980s, which raised great hopes of federal union only to let them down later. The failure of the grotesque European constitutional project launched in 2005, followed by the current decade of economic misery caused by the deeply flawed single currency debacle, has brought the EU to the sorry state of the present.

It is hardly surprising that the public remains ignorant of the workings of the Brussels administrative machinery. It has sweeping pretentions but little actual power and is operationally opaque. An early confrontation between the EU's executive, the Commission, and President de Gaulle resulted in a crushing defeat of Brussels—gave a *de facto* veto to each of the member states—and condemned the executive authority to two decades of frustration. Brussels' tireless campaign to centralize authority in Europe's so-called capital city also encountered dogged resistance from national business interests and bureaucracies, as well as labor unions. Sovereignty would remain firmly vested in the member states.

In the absence of both political accountability and a robust constitutional framework, the fledgling Eurocracy soon began to metastasize into congeries of agencies, committees, councils, boards, authorities of one kind another, projects, special purpose entities, and quangos, many of them not treaty-based. While most such aspirational bodies were mere shells, others of little initial importance would subsequently develop into powerhouses. For example, the European Court of Justice, set up to serve as an administrative tribunal, nowadays has the trappings of a supreme court. Its technically binding though predictably prejudicial judgments are today the EU's most powerful lever of influence.

Navigation of the euro-institutional maze presents a daunting task. Often described as a work in progress, and thus immune to definitive judgment, a meaningful description of the Brussels governance structure continues to elude scholars. The EU lacks essential attributes of statehood, according to the German public intellectual Josef Joffe, and in particular has no legitimizing foundation document equivalent to the American Constitution or, for that matter, to the unwritten British version of one. It is obvious that the EU is neither a genuine nation-state nor a true international organization but merely a hybrid transnational institution resting on murky legal foundations and with an ill-defined operational sphere.

Resorting to analogy, Joffe (2017) likens the EU organism—its structure, formation, and function—to that of a coral reef, something that is not a vegetable but not quite an animal, which grows under water but is only partly visible from the surface, is shapeless, and provides a living environment for species of small sea creatures like minnows and crabs: in other words, the diverse multitude of persons who cohabit under the rubric "European." It also shelters large beasts, the predators (presumably lobbyists and bureaucrats) who feed on them. Joffe might have added to his trope that coral reefs can only survive in special environments, lack mobility, and are—as their distressing disappearance makes evident—very fragile.

The EU has never had enough money or muscle to build a mass constituency with a vested interest in the growth of the welfare state. Instead, its power has expanded by dint of a Eurocratization process—the subsidizing of a powerful new hardcore intellectual policy-making elite, surrounded by soft-core outriders in the press, academia, and the chattering classes that still can be easily mobilized to influence the political process. Particular importance in this respect attaches to the Monnet-inspired think-tank, the Action Committee for the United States of Europe, many of whose prominent alumni, among them Valery Giscard d'Estaing and Helmut Schmidt, would later figure as keepers of the flame.

The clamorous voices of this institutionalized intellectual lobby have drowned out nearly all others and led to profound misunderstanding of the European integration process. This is not the place to attack this dominant quasi-official orthodoxy—those interested in the subject can read my books—but merely to state that its main conclusions, as propagated in the academic literature and much of the media, are widely off the mark and have led to basic—and very damaging—misconceptions.

The EU has not developed teleologically into a political union or anything like one. Its operations are hardly efficient and effective. It has not strengthened but undermined the legitimacy of representative government and done almost nothing to strengthen the welfare state. It is no agent of progress but a drag on it and is replaceable. And, as now evident to even the fiercest advocates, the EU is failing badly. Its would-be saviors should therefore be at least open to considering institutional reform instead of defending an untenable status quo.

An analysis of an important episode in the early history of the EEC/EU—of a path not taken—may shed light on a possible solution to present problems. Running parallel to the Messina negotiations that resulted in the Treaty of Rome and the EEC was another set of talks, led despondently by Britain, for a Free Trade Area (FTA). Whereas the EEC was designed as a customs union with a common external tariff, the FTA proposal merely eliminated tariff barriers between member states. A salient potential difference between the two was that whereas the EEC made provision for a political executive and restricted membership to the ECSC Six, the FTA was open to all Marshall Plan nations and had no explicit political objectives.

The skirmish lines in the competition between the EEC and the FTA were not clearly drawn. Contemporary European public opinion, to the extent that it can be fathomed by the surveys made at the time, favored "going with Britain," rather than "going with the Germans," a preference marked most clearly in France. While a bystander to both sets of talks, the United States encouraged The Six from behind the scenes and in effect favored diplomatic rapprochement over economic liberalization.

What sealed the fate of the FTA was a decision of the German Chancellor, the Francophile Konrad Adenauer, to override the preference of his economically liberal Minister of Economics Ludwig Erhard and come down in favor of the EEC. Also critical was the lack of effective British advocacy, especially the failure to argue the case for the FTA on economic principle, proving the British to be no less bound by the reigning corporatist orthodoxy than any of the others.

The single most important dissenter to the conventional wisdom policy was the Federal Republic's Economics Minister Ludwig Erhard. Erhard had been an odd duck in the Third Reich, a staff economist in an organization representing consumer interests. His political rise in postwar Germany was unscripted. He owed his prominence to the extraordinary success of the 1948 currency reform, a policy still revered as the symbolic birth act of the Federal Republic.

Erhard was a thoroughgoing free trader, whose then almost heretical policies proved that a unilateral absence of tariffs on imports could indeed trigger an "Economic Miracle." His approach derived from a specifically German school of thought, *ORDO*-liberalism, which regarded competition as essential both to democracy and to the breakup of the state capitalist system inherited from the Nazis. Like the leading light of the *ORDO* school, Wilhelm Röpke, Erhard aspired to a future Germany that would resemble "another Belgium"—economically strong but militarily weak. This was a notion Germany's neighbors could only have applauded.

An FTA victory in the contest with the future EU would have altered Europe's future. It would have been a more inclusive and representative organization than the EEC, would not have been bound by a Franco-German duopoly or built on the state-corporatist traditions of the trans-Rhenish powers, and would have been more open to competition as well as, in general, economic liberalization. Such a free trade area almost surely would have more closely resembled the conditions posited by Friedrich Hayek, in his seminal article, "The Economic Conditions of Interstate Federalism," than the course actually followed.

Hayek argued that open markets and political union go hand in hand—are both co-dependent and co-evolutionary—and that the absence of trade barriers prevents an identity of economic and political interests. The interplay of representative institutions and untrammeled competition reduces the power of governments to make economically discriminatory policy. The weakening of state authority in a federal union, it follows, would result in the devolution, through the marketplace, of decision-making to the regional and local level, where a bottoms-up approach would encourage innovation, stimulate growth, and invigorate democracy. This, then, is the liberal integration project that was not to be because of the dead weight of past practice and the institutional politics of the EEC/EU.

If an FTA-like organization is to revive the integration process in the future, it will have to wrest ownership of the term "integration" from EU orthodoxy, separate the study of it from the Brussels institutions, and consider more broadly how the process has really developed. One could do worse than to begin with Gottfried Haberler's (1964) inaugural address in 1963 as president of the American Economic Association, "Integration and Growth of the World Economy in Historical Perspective."

According to Haberler, there was nothing essentially new about post-WWII integration; rather it represented the most recent of three great waves in a long-term trend, the first of which took place at the national level beginning with the trade expansion of the eighteenth century, the second of which occurred internationally, through free trade in the nineteenth century, and the third of which is associated with the increasing economies of scale, which began after 1945.

Haberler took comfort in the fact that world trade had grown at a record rate of 6% annually in the 1950s and 1960s. He attributed these gains to the removal of direct and indirect "shackles" dating from the war as well as the restrictive regulations of the 1920s and 1930s. He concluded that (up to 1965) "the quantitative effects of trade on worldwide integration and liberalization have been much greater than those of the much more discussed and advertised regional schemes [of the predecessors of the EU]" (Haberler 1964).

Haberler's concept of integration as an historical and international phenomenon opens the way to a more sophisticated appreciation of those powerful forces and trends that brought about a closer union of Europe's peoples in the 1950s and 1960s. The list is long, exogenous rather than EU-specific, and it includes the interaction of both "hard" and "soft" power, but it can only be, in effect, penciled in at this point. It includes the Cold War threat of nuclear annihilation; the organizational context of international institutions that sprung from the Marshall Plan and NATO; and the Americanization of European taste, fashions, values, and culture.

Driving it were advanced technologies supported by new business institutions like the London euro-dollar market, the multinational corporation, and the big international American banks. Such developments in turn stimulated European imitation. In brief, the rise of a new consumer economy during the prosperous "twenty glorious years" of the 1950s and 1960s far outweighed the integrative importance of any single European institution, the same is true today and will continue to be so tomorrow.

The most powerful motor of integration is, as Haberler emphasizes, marketplace competition: its force can be temporarily thwarted but ultimately—and short of catastrophe—not be bottled up. It is a lesson the EU must learn if the decline of Europe is to be held in check as the world enters into a new era of high technology and competition with China. The obsolescence of the EU has long been evident, but no new design for it has been forthcoming or is palpably emerging from what the Columbia historian Adam Tooze (2019) calls the crude "calculus of power and material constraints"—nor likely will it in the absence of the big ideas that one associates with great thinkers like Hayek or Keynes. In the meantime, one could do worse than to re-examine the FTA alternative for insight into how Europeans might retrieve what is at once most honorable in the EU's history and which at the same time provides a welcome response to the formidable challenges of the present and future.

References

Haberler, Gottfried. 1964. Integration and Growth of the World Economy in Historical Perspective. *The American Economic Review* 54: 1–22.

Joffe, Josef. 2017. Nation and State vs. Europe: When the Sum of the Parts Is Larger Than the Whole. Lecture Delivered at the Institute of European Studies-University of California on October 16. Accessed May 29, 2020. https://ies.berkeley.edu/blog/nation-and-state-vs-europe-when-sum-parts-larger-whole.

Tooze, Adam. 2019. Everything You Know About Global Order Is Wrong. *Foreign Policy*, January 30. Accessed May 29, 2020. https://foreignpolicy.com/2019/01/30/everything-you-know-about-global-order-is-wrong/.

PART II

The Evolution of the European Project in the 1980s: How Liberalization Affected Europe

CHAPTER 8

The Re-launching of European Integration in the 1980s, Ideas and Policies

Jacques de Larosière

Two major developments (or undercurrents) have deeply affected the EEC in the 1980s. First, was the global move toward deregulation, which is in part the result of Thatcher's and Reagan's policies: Price and exchange controls were removed throughout the advanced world, financial markets became more open and integrated and the "Washington consensus" took hold. This consensus was, in particular, based on two, in my view questionable, beliefs: Financial market integration is favorable to economic growth and is better achieved through the "lightest" possible regulation, and markets are basically rational and tend to return rather quickly to balance when they get too far from fundamental values. Second, was the breakdown of the Soviet Empire in 1989.

The first structural move (deregulation and worldwide integration of financial markets) was a challenge for the EEC. Countries like France, which had a long tradition of exchange controls—French political parties (be they socialist or conservative) have always been tempted by *dirigisme*—had to adapt and align their financial policies and regulations to

J. de Larosière (✉)
Group of 30, Washington, DC, USA
e-mail: jacques.delarosiere@bnpparibas.com

F. Giavazzi et al. (eds.), *The Liberal Heart of Europe*,
https://doi.org/10.1007/978-3-030-60368-7_8

their more "open" neighbors, such as the UK, Germany, and Northern European countries. For the Community as a whole, the move toward deregulation accelerated the "internationalization" of European markets and their integration into the "Atlantic" world.

Paradoxically, deregulation—which was not in the main EEC tradition—became a factor of European integration: a new "paradigm" had been established. And the independence of central banks—as well as monetarism—became a common objective. In a way, the UK—newcomer after 1973—had won the debate between liberalism and *dirigisme*.

German unification had also a major impact on the EEC. The traditional "Franco-German couple" still kept its *raison d'être*, but its balance had changed. Germany was no more a "diplomatic dwarf": it had recovered influence and clout: it had become "more central" in the couple.

So, the situation had changed: the "traditional" European Economic Community was abandoning most of its administrative controls, reducing its deficit spending policies, timidly moving into supply-side policies and embracing inflation targeting, while the champion of a dynamic "social liberalism"—Germany—was getting more prominent and UK was doing well (notably productivity-wise).

Jacques Delors, President of the Commission (1985–1994), took advantage of the opportunities offered by this new environment. He threw his weight into "more European integration": A policy leading to a comprehensive single market to be achieved by 1992 under a "social and centralized" inspiration—more than a free trade objective. He played an important role in the creation of a European Monetary Union (Delors 1989). The—half-baked—idea was that an integrated common market had to be accompanied by a common currency. But this Delors architecture produced negative reactions especially in the UK. His three mottos were: *competition* that stimulates, *cooperation* that reinforces, *solidarity* that unites. In February 1986, an enlarged 12-member Europe, with the addition of Spain and Portugal, signed the Single Market Agreement which was a breakthrough, if only for introducing a majority-driven process of decision making in Europe.

One could argue that the EEC had embraced the deregulation and free capital market consensus—even Mitterrand to a large extent, after "*le tournant de la rigueur*." But the global increasing indebtedness was getting out of control, while structural weaknesses—combined with expensive social safety nets—especially in a number of non-core EU countries—were becoming the source of grave vulnerabilities which appeared later on.

In a way, the EEC-EU had had eyes bigger than stomach. Many imprecisions have remained: let me give a few examples. The name of the game in terms of the Single Market *was convergence of national regulations*, but in fact, legal options and national barriers still offered member countries a wide freedom to keep national rules—this was one of the reasons for the 2009 Financial Supervision Report, which I chaired.

Economic policy convergence was supposed to be the cornerstone of the Maastricht Monetary Union. But, in fact, convergence was weak and only really started, because of market pressure, ten years after the beginning of the euro. (Those ten first years of divergence were the cause of the 2010 sovereign crisis.)

Solidarity mechanisms have proven to be weak and not sufficient to help a more balanced adjustment system within the EMU between creditors and debtor countries: Present imbalances in the Union are far from being only created by "bad behavior from the southern periphery." Little by little, *the more or less implicit "common view" led to rather different interpretations between the Commission and some member states* (on social and financial solidarity, fiscal policies, stronger centralized norms, etc.) This resulted inevitably in future, dramatic reactions and divergences among states. More generally, the way the Commission works—by trying pragmatic *ad hoc* compromises between member states, while not being able in many cases to refer to a common strategic anchor—leads inevitably to opportunistic moves and to ambiguity, or even contradictions, between words and facts.

Reference

Delors, Jacques. 1989. *Report on Economic and Monetary Union in the European Community*. Report presented by the Committee for the Study of Economic and Monetary Union, April 17. Accessed May 29, 2020. http://aei.pitt.edu/1007/1/monetary_delors.pdf.

CHAPTER 9

Evaluating Mrs. Thatcher's Reforms: Britain's 1980s Economic Reform Program

Patrick Minford

The aims of Margaret Thatcher's reform program were to cure the "British Disease" of the 1970s: low growth, high inflation, and high unemployment. It had two main elements: "monetarism" (namely monetary policy and complementary fiscal policy to defeat inflation) and "supply-side policy." This last in turn consisted of two main components: labor market flexibility to reduce unemployment, and the reduction of barriers to entrepreneurial activity (taxes and regulations), to raise productivity growth.

These reforms were deliberately sequenced for practical political reasons—see Minford (1998) for more details on these policies.

Monetarism and the defeat of inflation came first. Then, starting in her second term, Mrs. Thatcher embarked on her supply-side program, which would then also occupy her third term. A key element that helped her in the supply-side reforms was that, inflation having been defeated, demand policy was reasonably free to support them.

P. Minford (✉)
Cardiff Business School, Cardiff University, Cardiff, UK
e-mail: minfordp@cf.ac.uk

F. Giavazzi et al. (eds.), *The Liberal Heart of Europe*,
https://doi.org/10.1007/978-3-030-60368-7_9

9.1 The Monetarist Program

The program to defeat inflation, then running at close to 20%, was formulated as a "gradualist" one, following advice from Milton Friedman (explained in Friedman 1980). It would reduce both the growth of £M_3 (a proxy for bank credit) and the fiscal deficit as a share of GDP—the latter included (against Friedman's advice) to ensure credibility of the monetary target, as emphasized in rational expectations models. In the event, "the best-laid plans *gang agley*" and both these targets were substantially overshot, as Figs. 9.1 and 9.2 show. The recession was the cause of the overshoot in both. The deficit (measured here by the public sector borrowing requirement, PSBR) surged as welfare benefits rose and revenues fell with falling GDP and rising unemployment. Bank credit and so £M_3, the chosen indicator, grew rapidly as firms hit by falling receipts borrowed heavily from the banks to stay in business; the Bank of England, which was

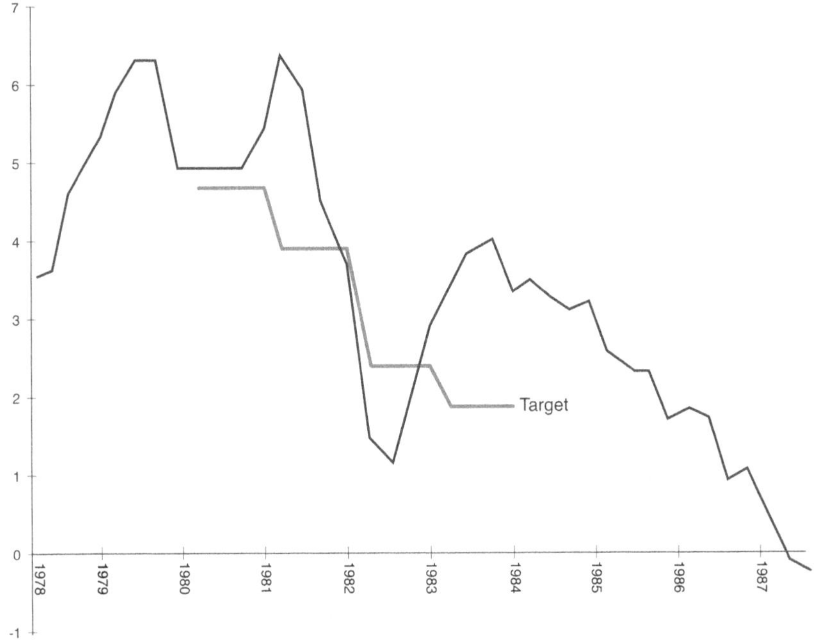

Fig. 9.1 PSBR/GDP 4 quarter average. (*Source*: Adapted in simplified form from Minford 1998, Fig. 4.5)

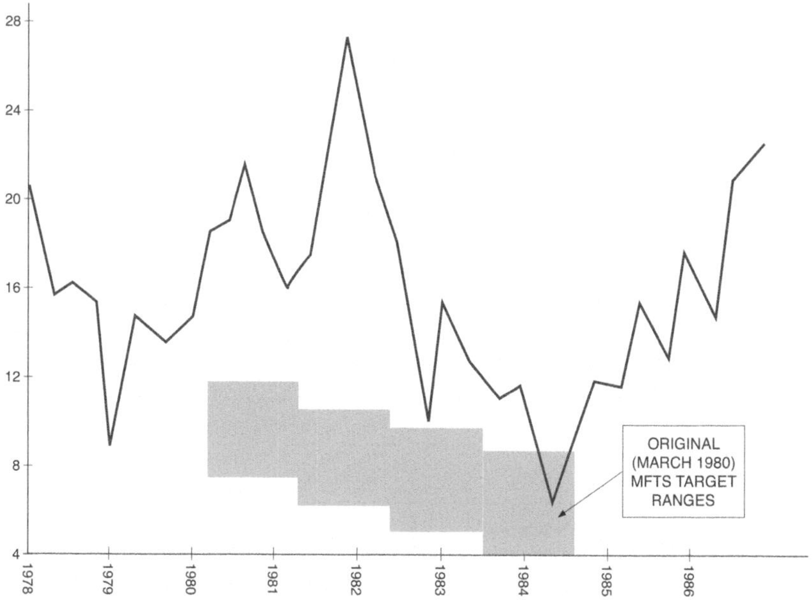

Fig. 9.2 Annual percentage growth in £M_3. (*Source*: Adapted in simplified form from Minford 1998, Fig. 4.6)

opposed to monetarist policies, lent supportively to the banks to facilitate this.

Faced with these overshoots, the government could have abandoned the policies and accepted defeat. However, instead Mrs. Thatcher pressed on, insisting that the money supply and budget deficits would be curbed to ensure the defeat of inflation, whatever the short-term pain. The main focus was on fiscal policy: the fiscal stance was tightened in the 1981 budget to boost policy credibility. As long-run interest rates came down, it also permitted a cut in interest rates on the grounds that monetary conditions as measured by money supply indicators other than the chosen one were in fact rather too tight—see Fig. 9.3 of M_4.

As is well known, the critical 1981 budget attracted strong criticism in the famous *Times Letter* from 364 economists: The mass of UK economists, who generally opposed the policies, preferring price/wage controls and demand stimulus, argued that the policies would create long-running recession, with little if any effect on inflation (Booth 2006).

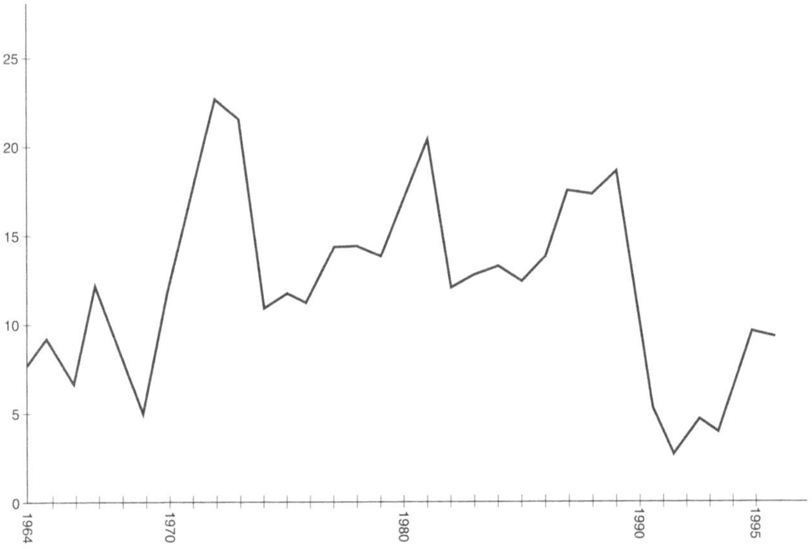

Fig. 9.3 M_4 growth. (*Source*: Adapted in simplified form from Minford 1998, Fig. 4.10)

However, they were wrong, as Fig. 9.4 of inflation shows. By the end of 1982 inflation had fallen below 5%. Furthermore, growth in 1982 picked up sharply, signaling the end of the recession. Unemployment stayed high, but it became plain that this was not through lack of demand, but because of supply-side problems in the labor market: real wages were being held at unrealistically high levels by unconditionally provided unemployment benefits and powerful unions. Also manufacturing productivity was low, after years of subsidies and loose control of credit. It became clear that the supply-side program must be ushered in.

9.2 The Supply-Side Reforms, Part One: Labor Market Flexibility

The first part of the program was focused on labor market flexibility. The unemployment benefits/wage ratio was curbed; eligibility for these benefits was made conditional on proper search, to be monitored in job market interviews at the benefit office under a "Restart" review. Union strike

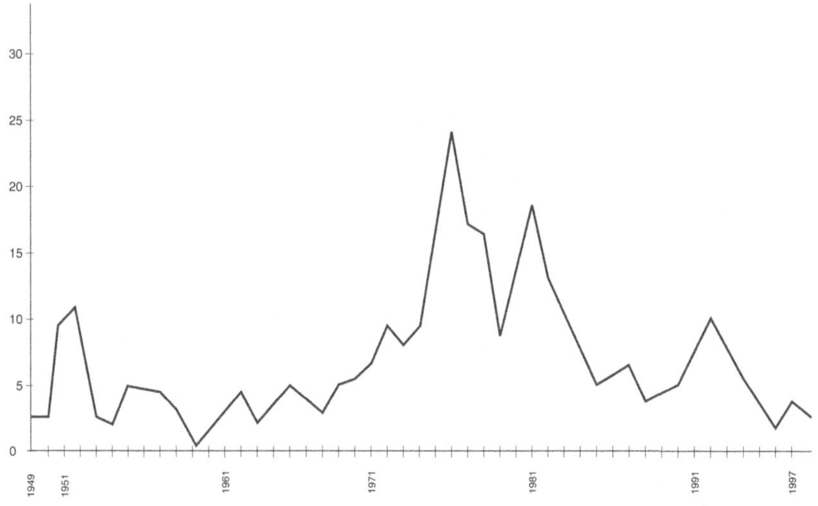

Fig. 9.4 RPI inflation—all items. (*Source*: Adapted in simplified form from Minford 1998, Fig. 4.3)

powers were cut back: strikes would be permitted only after a full members' ballot and only over the pay/conditions of members—no "secondary action" would be allowed, that is, strikes by other workers in suppliers or customers of the employing firm. Strikes in breach of these laws would not be protected against tort contract violation by existing "union immunities" (these allowed unions to "induce contract violation" legally); so civil court action against unions over illegal strikes could and did lead to large-scale damages and fines. These measures proved to be highly effective in curbing strikes and lowering incentives to avoid job search—see Figs. 9.5 and 9.6. Figure 9.6 on the benefit/wage ratio relates to the basic benefit for a low-paid worker where unemployment was concentrated. In addition, there was an earnings-related supplement for higher-paid workers; this was abolished in 1982. Strong conditionality on paying benefits was also introduced in 1986 under the "Restart" process. Figure 9.7 shows both actual unemployment and the estimates from the Liverpool supply-side model of the UK for the natural/equilibrium unemployment rate emerging from these reforms. It can be seen that by the end of the 1980s both actual and equilibrium unemployment had fallen greatly. Actual unemployment was to rise again sharply at the start of the 1990s,

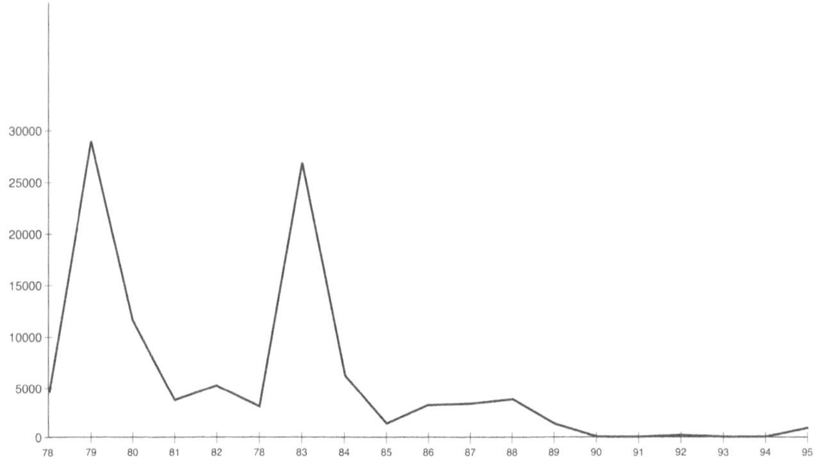

Fig. 9.5 Working days lost in strikes. (*Source*: Adapted in simplified form from Minford 1998, Fig. 5.2)

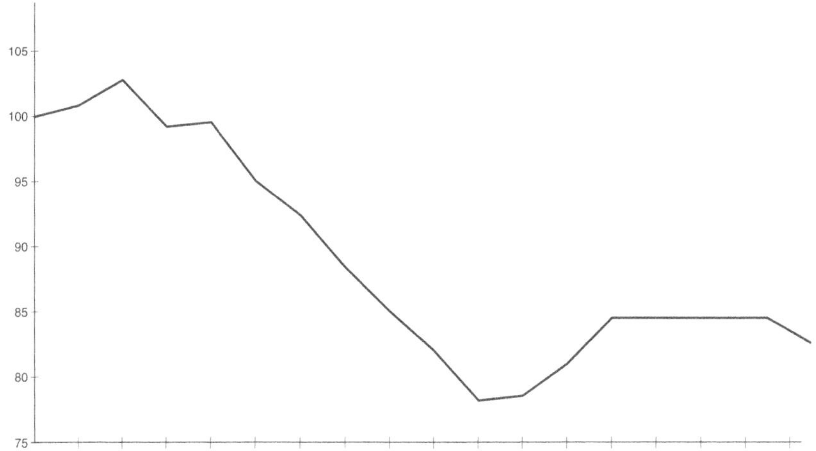

Fig. 9.6 Benefits—excluding earning-related supplement—relative to real wages (1980 = 100). (*Source*: Adapted in simplified form from Minford 1998, Fig. 5.3)

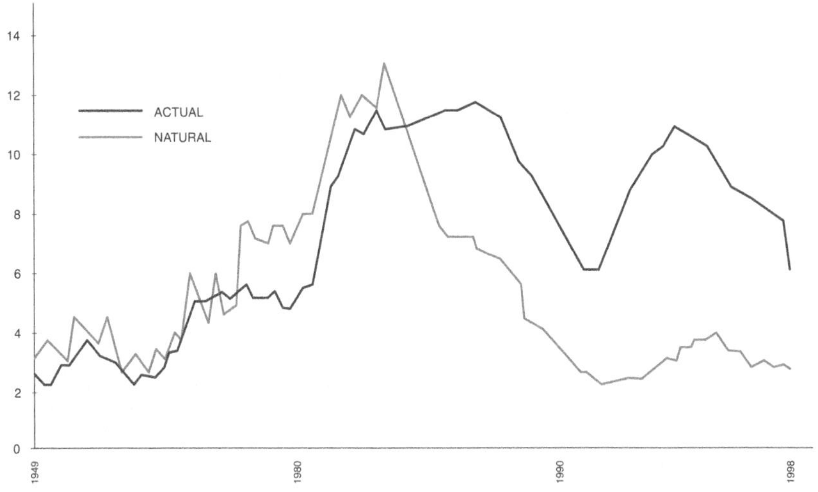

Fig. 9.7 Actual and natural rates of unemployment. (*Source*: Adapted in simplified form from Minford 1998, Fig. 5.5)

as a result of recession associated with UK entry into the European Exchange Rate Mechanism in 1990, a serious policy mistake. But otherwise unemployment has been on a steady downward path to its latest rate of around 2% on the benefits-claimant measure used here.

9.3 The Supply-Side Reforms, Part Two: Improved Environment for Entrepreneurs

For entrepreneurial firms seeking to raise productivity, regulative intervention in the labor market, via union powers and social intervention (labor rights), was a major issue in pre-Thatcher Britain. Hence the labor market flexibility reforms just examined also constituted an important element in the improvement of the entrepreneurial environment. The other main element involved taxes on entrepreneurs: notably the top marginal income tax rates and corporation tax on SMEs.

It has proved difficult to find evidence of causal linkages between such business disincentives and productivity growth. There have been many studies showing that there is a statistical link between the two, but causation cannot be demonstrated by such studies (Minford et al. 2007).

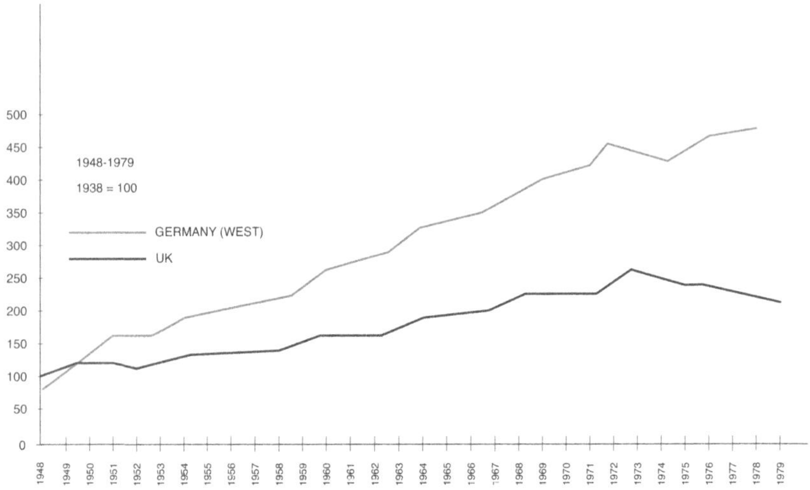

Fig. 9.8 Manufacturing productivity in Germany and the UK, 1948–79. (*Source*: Adapted in simplified form from Minford 1998, Fig. 3.9)

Figure 9.9 on UK manufacturing productivity growth and its comparison with West Germany shows the way relative productivity surged in the UK after 1979, as compared with the poor post-war performance up to 1979 (Fig. 9.8). But we need serious causal analysis to establish a link with the reforms.

In recent research (Minford 2015; Minford and Meenagh 2020) evidence of causation has been established. A model of the UK economy in which regulatory costs affect productivity growth is simulated to generate behavior of GDP and productivity, as well as other economic variables over the period from 1970 to 2009. If this model is a correct representation of the UK, then the behavior of the economy we actually observed in this period should be accounted for by these simulations. This work finds that one cannot reject this hypothesis statistically with 95% confidence.

First, we may inspect the data on tax and labor market regulation (LMR) in the UK over this period of the Thatcher reforms. In the left panel of Fig. 9.9 are three series: the top marginal income tax rate, the small company corporation tax rate, and LMR (mainly reflecting union laws). In Panel 2 are two series representing different weighted combinations of these, Tau(1) and Tau(2). For the main results Tau(1), which

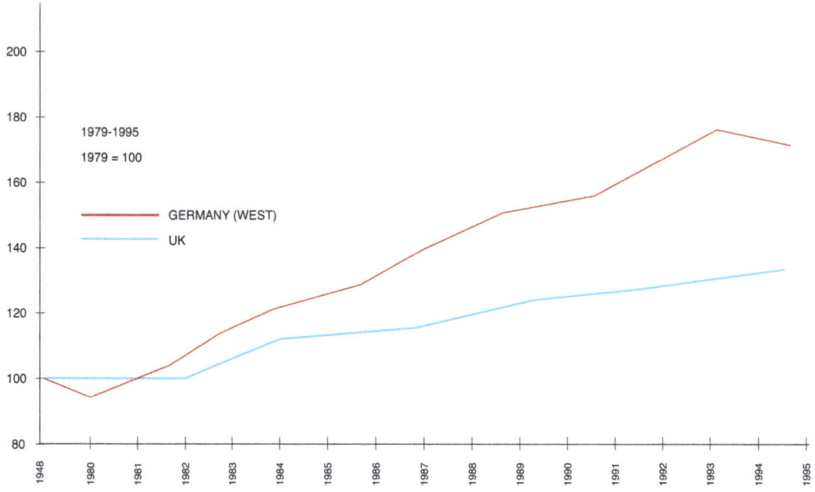

Fig. 9.9 Manufacturing productivity in Germany and the UK, 1979–95. (*Source*: Adapted in simplified form from Minford 1998, Fig. 3.9)

equally weights LMR and the top marginal rate, is used; however. the results are robust to using Tau(2), which replaces the top marginal rate with the corporate tax rate.

The method of testing involved here is indirect inference, checking whether the simulated behavior of the UK economy growth model was the same as its actual behavior. In this instance the behavior is relationships of output, productivity, and the tax/regulation variable. It turns out that the hypothesis the simulated behavior is the same as the actual has a *p*-value of 0.18, well above the 0.05 rejection threshold. Figures 9.10, 9.11, and 9.12 illustrate how similar the actual behavior and the average simulated behavior is for these variables; this underpins the similarity of the actual and the simulated relationships between them.

This work represents something of a breakthrough in the longstanding debate over causal evidence in this area. The specific effect of a sustained ten-year 5% rise in the measure of intervention (equivalent to a rise in the effective tax rate) on growth is for a fall in growth of 1.5% a year over two decades—about 30% in total. Over the 1980s the intervention measure (Tau in Fig. 9.9) fell between 5% and 20%, depending on which measure

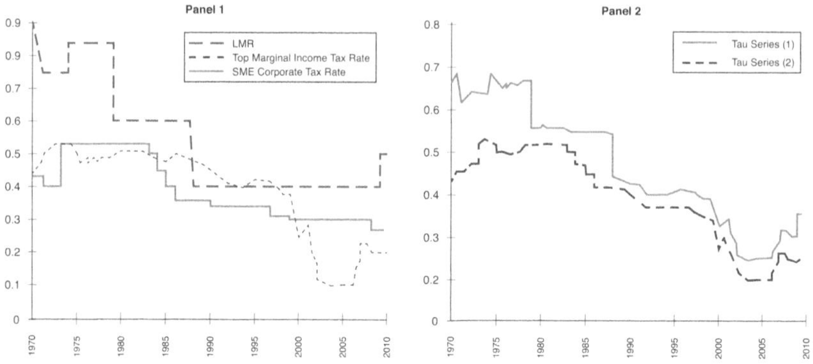

Fig. 9.10 Data on tax and labor market regulation (LMR) in the UK during the Thatcher reforms. (*Source*: Minford and Meenagh 2020, Fig. 2)

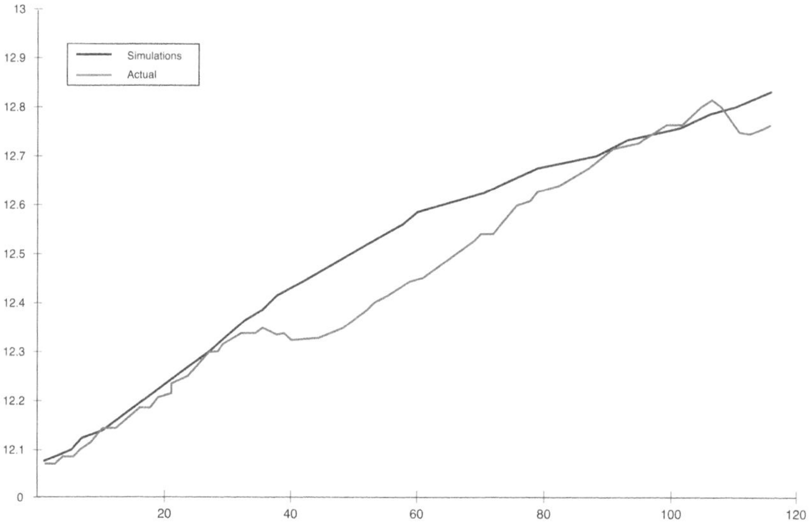

Fig. 9.11 Match of average simulated output to actual productivity. (*Source*: Minford and Meenagh 2020)

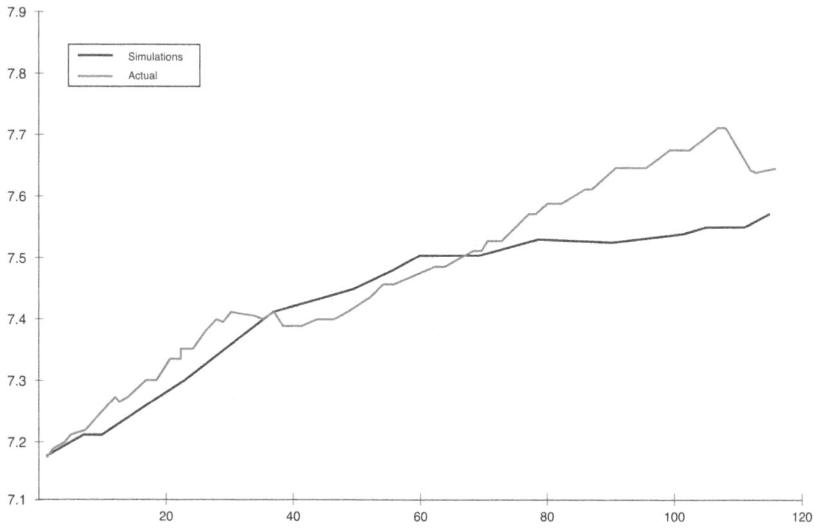

Fig. 9.12 Match of average simulated output to actual output. (*Source*: Minford and Meenagh 2020)

one uses: the effect on the growth rate of productivity could have been between 1.5% and 6% therefore. This is a substantial effect.

9.4 A Note on the Political Economy of Mrs. Thatcher's Reforms

One of the apparent puzzles of the Thatcher reforms is how they came to be politically possible, given the largescale forces arrayed against them. For a start, big business, as typified by the Confederation of British Industry (CBI), was against monetarism with its elimination of easy credit and the end of the associated devaluations. It was also against union reform, since unions acted as an effective entry barrier to new, especially SME, firms. Meanwhile of course unions and the political left were against the reduction in wage inflation and the curbing of union powers. The Tory party was split, with "one-nation Tories" opposed to the reforms, on all these grounds. This created a constant fear of leadership challenge within the Thatcher government. In response to this threat, Mrs. Thatcher put key economic portfolios in hands of trusted allies—Howe, Lawson, Ridley, and Tebbit. Her opponents, lacking economics expertise, found it hard to challenge this group on economic grounds.

The main support for Mrs. Thatcher came from the skilled working class, whose interests manual unions undermined, by pushing up manual wages and disrupting production at the expense of profits and so skilled wages. Adding to this support, the defeat of inflation was extremely popular: inflation, with its effects in redistributing resources to those lucky or smart enough to do well from inflation, had become highly unpopular. The other central policy of "bringing unions within the law" was also widely acclaimed.

However, the key element that buttressed Mrs. Thatcher's position was Tory Party compromise, faced with the threat of a far left-wing Labour government under Michael Foot. (A close parallel with today's recent threat of a Corbyn government.) Hence, the secret of the reforms' feasibility and success was the willingness of the Tory Party to maintain its power, to back the reform program and combine with its "new working class" support base. One of the main intermediaries between the Tory one-nation group and Mrs. Thatcher was William, later made Lord, Whitelaw, who explained these realities to his old-guard friends. In recording her gratitude to him for his efforts and loyalty in buttressing her governments, Mrs. Thatcher much later remarked, "Everyone needs a Willie." Needless to say, in spite of the ensuing hilarity, it was not a joke, and indeed jokes were not her style—rather she made remarks that were barbed with wit as when after a dinner celebrating the IEA's 50th anniversary in 2005 when speaking last after a long line-up of men she remarked slightly testily, "The cock may crow but it's the hen that lays the eggs."

9.5 Conclusions

The reform program of the Thatcher governments is widely regarded as a success story in curing the 1970s ailments—inflation, slow growth, and rising unemployment—of the British economy, then "the sick man of Europe." They began with UK monetarism, and followed with labor market reforms, and finally with the reshaping of taxes and government spending to help the rebirth of an entrepreneurial economy. The early monetarist phase was meant to be gradualist but mistakes delivered a very sharp squeeze; as people understood that the policy regime had changed, inflation fell far quickly and growth recovered. The labor market reforms brought down unemployment by raising work incentives; aided by falling tax rates the environment became propitious for entrepreneurs, raising productivity growth. Margaret Thatcher was able to assemble the support for this ambitious agenda to succeed politically against many opposing interests, because of the ability of the Conservative party to unite its traditional middle-class constituency with the newly emerging, aspiring skilled working-class constituency, which had a strong interest in these reforms.

References

Booth, Philip. 2006. *Were 364 Economists All Wrong?* London: Institute of Economic Affairs.

Friedman, Milton. 1980. Evidence. Memorandum: Response to Questionnaire on Monetary Policy. In *The House of Commons Treasury and Civil Service Committee: Memorandum on Monetary Policy. Great Britain, Parliamentary Papers (Commons), Session 1979-1980, 720, part 1 (July 1980), 1–4*, 55–61. London: Her Majesty's Stationary Office.

Minford, Patrick. 1998. *Markets not Stakes—The Triumph of Capitalism and The Stakeholder Fallacy*. London: Orion Business Books.

Minford, Lucy. 2015. *The Impact of Policy on UK Output and Productivity Growth, 1970–2009: Testing an Open Economy DSGE Model of the UK*. PhD thesis, Cardiff University. https://cronfa.swan.ac.uk/Record/cronfa34064. Accessed 1 June 2020.

Minford, Lucy, and David Meenagh. 2020. Supply-Side Policy and Economic Growth: A Case Study of the UK. *Open Economies Review* 31: 159–193. https://doi.org/10.1007/s11079-019-09536-8.

Minford, Patrick, David Meenagh, and Jiang Wang. 2007. *Growth and Relative Living Standards—Testing Barriers to Riches on Post-War Panel Data*. Working paper no. E2007/12. Cardiff: Cardiff University.

CHAPTER 10

The Rocky Road to European Monetary Union: A German Perspective

Otmar Issing

10.1 The Trauma of 1945

To understand the German attitude toward European integration one has to go back to 1945. The disaster of the Nazi regime and WWII had not only caused a total collapse of the economy but even destroyed any sense of national and moral identity. Luckily for Germany—until 1990 these considerations refer to West Germany—emerging tensions between the Allies and the Soviet Union created an interest in her recovery.

(Western) European integration, which started in 1950 with the Schuman Plan, and reconciliation between the former "arch-enemies" brought Germany into the camp of democracies. Atlantic ties and European integration established the political basis for Germany's astounding recovery. There was no *Wirtschaftswunder*, but the implementation of a market-friendly economic order and the introduction of the Deutsche Mark in 1948. For the first time in two generations, Germans enjoyed the benefits of a stable currency.

O. Issing (✉)
University of Würzburg, Würzburg, Germany
e-mail: wue@otmar-issing.de

F. Giavazzi et al. (eds.), *The Liberal Heart of Europe*,
https://doi.org/10.1007/978-3-030-60368-7_10

With her growing economic success, Germany soon together with France became a leader in European integration. Isn't it astonishing that in 1958 the first president of the European Commission was a German, Walter Hallstein?

10.2 Early Initiatives for European Monetary Union (EMU)

In December 1968, the European Summit in The Hague decided to establish a group tasked with drawing up a proposal for an economic and monetary union. In autumn 1970 the Werner Group, named after the prime minister of Luxembourg who chaired it, presented a report that essentially contained a plan for establishing economic and monetary union in three stages. A short time afterward, it was considered that this project should be completed over a period of ten years. For the whole process, see Tietmeyer (2005) and Szász (1999).

This overambitious aim was doomed to fail from the outset. The following period was marked by turbulence in foreign exchange markets. Attempts to stabilize exchange rates in Europe via the introduction of the "snake" had no lasting success. In Germany, the "economistic view" dominated, which held that the (premature) fixing of exchange rates without lasting convergence inevitably creates tensions that ultimately generate sudden, major exchange rate changes (Issing 2008). Convergence of monetary policy is a key requisite, but wage policy and fiscal policy have also to adapt to the regime of fixed exchange rates. This view was also shared by economists from other countries. In contrast, the "monetarist view" was popular in France. In a nutshell, the argument is: Once exchange rates are fixed, convergence of monetary policy is more or less bound to follow.

The former German Minister of Economic Affairs and Finance Karl Schiller was a strong supporter of the economistic view. Chancellor Helmut Schmidt was close to the French position and, together with President Giscard d'Estaing, fostered the project of a new exchange rate system. On the back of their initiative, the European Monetary System (EMS) was established and came into effect on March 13, 1979.

The EMS is characterized as follows:

- The European Currency Unit (ECU), a currency basket, was formally the center of the system.

- Exchange rates were fixed between the member currencies (the parity grid).
- Compulsory interventions were correspondingly tied not to the ECU but to the parity grid.

For Giscard and Schmidt, the EMS was a project going far beyond the merits of an exchange rate system (Szász 1999). As it turned out, the ECU played a much more limited role (e.g. as a unit of account). It soon became apparent that the EMS was a system founded on its strongest currency—in short, it was a "DM bloc" (Issing 2008).

It didn't take long before the new system came under heavy strain. The second oil price shock of 1979–1980 exerted strong price pressure, which represented a great challenge for macroeconomic policy. Not least because of the negative experience of the first oil price shock, when inflation rose sharply, this time the Bundesbank decided to nip inflationary pressures in the bud. As a consequence, Germany escaped from the "Great inflation" (Issing 2005). In comparison to the US, for example, the credible commitment of the Bundesbank to its goal of price stability spared Germany a repetition of the sequence of inflation and stagflation that had marked the period after the first oil price shock (Issing et al. 2013). Within the EMS, the Bundesbank became the leader in the fight against inflation. Those countries that were unable or unwilling to join in this disinflationary process were forced into repeated devaluations of their currencies after their attempts to defend parities had reached crisis point. The other members faced a de facto choice: either follow the monetary policy of the Bundesbank or devalue their currencies.

10.3 German Reunification: A Dramatic Shock

The Wall, which had divided Germany into a democracy with a market economy in the West and a communist dictatorship with a planned economy in the East, fell on November 9, 1989. German monetary union was established less than a year later, on June 1, 1990, and political union achieved on October 3 of the same year. This was a unique historical event. Economically, it implied a dramatic shock. The macroeconomic dimension is marked by Germany transforming from a net exporter of capital with a corresponding current account surplus into a large net importer of capital with a deficit in the current account. Between 1989 and 1992, the swing in the current account amounted to almost 150 billion DM, which was roughly 5% of pan-German GDP (see Issing 1993). The swing in the trade balance was over 100 billion DM, which implied an increase in real imports of almost 30%. In the first years of this period the number of new cars imported rose by more than 75%—which implied a substantial positive real shock to some partner countries.

Germany's reunification had turned almost all economic relations upside down. Huge budget (and off-budget) deficits were just one consequence. The rapid increase in the share of public expenditure of GDP within a few years, from 46.5% in 1989 to (roughly) 54.5% in 1993, probably gives an overall impression of the dimension of the macroeconomic shock. However, for the people of the former German Democratic Republic (GDR), the new regime represented an unprecedented challenge that is still ongoing today—but this is another story.

I had joined the Bundesbank in October 1990 and it was my responsibility to present the monetary target for the next year. My first initiative was to warn my staff that this was no time for business as usual. As a consequence, the first and fundamental question was whether the Bundesbank should stick to its so-far successful strategy. Monetary policy is always exposed to uncertainty. But this was a case of sailing in uncharted waters (Issing 2005). Introducing the DM in the still existing GDR was a logistical masterstroke. However, the generous conversion of *Ostmark* holdings into DM led to a 15% increase in the money supply. The national product of the former GDR (estimated with a high degree of uncertainty) implied that a noninflationary increase in the money stock of only 10% would have been warranted. Besides, how would the new citizens of this united Germany adjust to the new regime? What were the consequences for potential output growth, for the velocity of money circulation? And finally, should the Bundesbank keep its normative inflation rate of 2% unchanged? These three elements for deriving the monetary target were all marked by high uncertainty.

To summarize: Despite the unusual dimension of the shock caused by German unification, the Bundesbank decided that abandoning the strategy of monetary targeting might be interpreted as a sign of surrender to these huge challenges.

The Bundesbank had always followed a strategy of "pragmatic monetarism" (Issing 1996), which implied that it would not resort to extreme measures to keep the growth rate within the announced range. The focus was on the medium term and specifically on keeping price developments in line with the stability mandate. This strategy came under extreme strain when fiscal deficits rose dramatically, wages soared, and inflation (in West Germany) rose above 4%. The target for the broad monetray aggregate M_3 in 1992 was 3.5 to 5.5%. But M_3 increased in the first quarter of 1992, for example, by an annual rate of 9% (Issing 1992a). Against the background of persistent inflationary risks and the acceleration of M_3 growth, the governing council had raised both the Lombard and discount rates by 0.5 percentage point each to the record level of 9.75% and 8% in December 1991. The Bundesbank's determination to defend price stability, even in such a unique historical situation, saved Germany from a potential loss of credibility in the stability of the DM. Inflationary expectations remained under control and long-term interest rates stabilized. In the course of the following years, M_3 growth returned to the target range and price increases gradually moderated. This is the domestic side.

This period caused extreme strain on the EMS. The huge turbulences in foreign exchange markets in 1992 and 1993 with dramatic realignments—the DM appreciated by more than 30% against the Italian lira—put even the achievement of the Single Market at risk.

Such extreme turbulence could have been avoided if other countries had agreed to a timely realignment of exchange rates. The mandate of the Bundesbank to maintain price stability was clearly a domestic one. Yet, the Bundesbank's policy also carried a positive European dimension. As was earlier explained, the DM played the role of an anchor for price stability within the EMS. A monetary policy of the Bundesbank temporarily neglecting its stability mandate until the shock of unification had been mitigated—as had been suggested also in Germany—would have been a dangerous signal for the future monetary union. The DM acted as an anchor also during the convergence process toward EMU (see Issing and Masuch 1992). Without this role, it would have been impossible for the European Central Bank to start its monetary policy in an environment of price stability with an implied transfer of credibility from the Bundesbank to the new European institution. "Not least in this respect, there is no conflict in the Bundesbank`s policy between the fulfillment of its national tasks and its international, in particular European, commitments" (Issing 1992b).

10.4 German Reunification and European Monetary Integration

There exists a widespread belief that giving up the DM was the price that had to be paid to gain approval for German reunification from its partners. It is certainly true that not all European governments were happy about the idea of German reunification. The French President Mitterrand was among the skeptics—to say the least—and the British Prime Minister Thatcher openly opposed such plans (Tietmeyer 2005, p. 139). It cannot be denied that German reunification raised concerns about a much more powerful Germany now representing a much higher population; previously the three largest countries were roughly equally populated. Against this background, giving up such a precious national asset as the DM was seen as a strong sign of Germany's willingness to become even more closely bound to Europe. Chancellor Kohl, in particular, repeated this mantra time and again. He saw German reunification and further European integration as "two sides of the same coin" (Tietmeyer 2005, p. 140).

However, preparations for monetary union had started well before the fall of the Wall. They began with initiatives in France in January 1989 and in Italy in February 1989, followed by a personal memorandum by the German Foreign Minister Genscher, which came as a surprise to the German government as well as the Bundesbank—for a history of these events, see Tietmeyer (2005) and Szász (1999). A month later Finance Minister Stoltenberg, in cooperation with the Bundesbank, gained control of the development. His memorandum of March 15, 1989, documented the traditional German "economistic position," emphasizing the importance of reducing inflation and budget deficits as well as liberalizing capital movements between partner countries before considering monetary integration.

The Committee of Central Bank Governors and the Delors Group presented reports on a future European Central Bank and a common currency. After numerous consultations, the European Council, at its meeting of June 26–27, 1989, in Madrid, decided to initiate the first stage of the European Economic and Monetary Union in 1990 by liberalizing the movement of capital.

There is no doubt that the decision to move toward European monetary union was taken before the fall of the Wall. Ultimately, German reunification added momentum to a journey that had already begun.

10.5 Conclusion

As was previously explained, the DM played a dominant role within the EMS and other countries had to either follow the policy of the Bundesbank or devalue their currencies from time to time. To stick to the course of the Bundesbank was seen as beneficial in countries like the Netherlands and Austria. For France it was hard, and in the longer run unacceptable, to have its monetary policy "made in Frankfurt" (at that time by the Bundesbank). The DM was even characterized as Germany's "nuclear weapon." Since all attempts to share the responsibility for monetary policy with existing national currencies had failed, France finally accepted the idea of a European central bank and a common currency. As it was clear that Germany would insist on a statute for the future European central bank based on independence and priority for price stability, all participating countries finally signed such a statute in Maastricht, at a time when their national central banks did not enjoy independence.

A kind of a strong mental reservation in France is expressed in the words of President Mitterrand in a television debate on September 3, 1992, in the run-up to the French referendum on the Maastricht Treaty: "La Banque Centrale, la future Banque Central ... elle ne decide pas ... Les techniciens de la Banque Centrale sont chargés d'appliquer dans la domaine monétaire les décisions du Conseil Européen, prises par les douze Chefs d'Etat et de Gouvernement, c'est-à-dire par les politiques qui représentent leurs peuples ..." (Issing 2008, p. 59).

Concerns in Germany were of a very different nature. The Bundesbank expressed its satisfaction that the statute of the future European central bank was largely in line with the Bundesbank's recommendation. The bank emphasized that the convergence criteria should be strictly applied in the selection of countries that would qualify. The Bundesbank also insisted on steps in the direction of a political union. But this is another long story.

References

Issing, Otmar. 1992a. The National and International Responsibility of German Monetary Policy Makers. *Auszüge aus Presseartikeln* 36, May 20. Frankfurt am Mein: Deutsche Bundesbank.

———. 1992b. German Unification and European Integration—Challenges for the Bundesbank's Monetary Policy. *Auszüge aus Presseartikeln* 42, June 16. Frankfurt am Mein: Deutsche Bundesbank.

———. 1993. Gesamtwirtschaftliche Folgen des deutschen Einigungsprozesses. *Auszüge aus Presseartikeln* 55, August 11. Frankfurt am Mein: Deutsche Bundesbank.

———. 1996. Is Monetary Targeting in Germany Still Adequate? In *Monetary Policy in an Integrated World Economy: Symposium 1995*, ed. Horst Siebert, 117–130. Tübingen: J.C.B. Mohr.

———. 2005. Why Did the Great Inflation Not Happen in Germany? *Federal Reserve Bank of St. Louis Review* 87: 329–335. Accessed June 23, 2020. https://files.stlouisfed.org/files/htdocs/publications/review/05/03/part2/Issing.pdf.

———. 2008. *The Birth of the Euro*. Cambridge, UK: Cambridge University Press.

Issing, Otmar, and Klaus Masuch. 1992. EWS, Währungsunion und Kapitalallokation. Neue Perspektiven durch die deutsche Wiedervereinigung. In *Währungspolitische Probleme im integrierten Europa*, ed. Claus Köhler and Rüdiger Pohl, 37–62. Berlin: Duncker & Humblot.

Issing, Otmar, Andreas Beyer, Vítor Gaspar, and Christina Gerberding. 2013. Opting Out of the Great Inflation: German Monetary Policy after the Breakdown of Bretton Woods. In *The Great Inflation: The Rebirth of Modern Central Banking*, ed. Michael D. Bordo and Athanasios Orphanides, 301–346. Chicago and London: NBER.

Szász, André. 1999. *The Road to European Monetary Union*. Houndmills, Basingstoke, and London: Palgrave Macmillan Press.

Tietmeyer, Hans. 2005. *Herausforderung EURO. Wie es zum Euro kam und was es für Deutschlands Zukunft bedeutet*. München: Carl Hanser Verlag.

PART III

Our Current Predicament

CHAPTER 11

The Euro in Perspective

John B. Taylor

Just before the introduction of the euro, I was invited by Otmar Issing to come to Frankfurt to discuss the problems of monetary policy with a new currency. Otmar Issing often recalls that discussion, and I can say that it was fascinating to have had the chance to offer some advice on that visit, but also to be at the first "ECB and Its Watchers" conference in 1999 and at several later ones. Today, two decades later, I want to consider the euro in perspective—both an historical and a global perspective—based on what we have experienced in the years since then, but without the special changes brought on by the pandemic that began in 2020.

11.1 Successes

Many successes have been rightly associated with the introduction of the euro and the creation of the European Central Bank (ECB). Early on, the ECB handled communication and transparency issues very well. That was certainly an area of concern of mine 20 years ago, when the diverse communications strategies of many national central banks, with different

J. B. Taylor (✉)
Hoover Institution, Stanford University, Stanford, CA, USA
e-mail: johnbtaylor@stanford.edu

F. Giavazzi et al. (eds.), *The Liberal Heart of Europe*,
https://doi.org/10.1007/978-3-030-60368-7_11

languages and widely different traditions, had to be carefully taken account of and integrated. Issing (2014) reviews the impressive innovations: the press conferences—including the introductory statement, questions and answers, public projections by the staff, and good connections with academics and banking economists through the watcher conferences. This was an amazing accomplishment, and much has been copied by other central banks, including the US Federal Reserve System (the Fed) as it now too uses post-meeting press conferences. Transparency and clear policy communications are hallmarks of economic systems that emphasize economic freedom.

The ECB has also been a voice for structural and market-based reforms in individual countries. Indeed, this is another good example of the idea that underlies this volume, that economic ideas are often more embraced by international bodies than by institutions in countries.

And while the euro has not become as much of an international currency as many had hoped, the ECB has gained respect as a transnational institution in Europe, perhaps more than the European Parliament and the European Commission.

From the beginning, there was of course the concern that a single currency regime could be a determent to economic stability compared to a flexible exchange rate regime, but there were few empirical studies which "attempted to evaluate the effects of fixed vs. flexible exchange rates … while dealing with expectational issues and capital mobility, both of which are widely viewed as crucial to exchange-rate behavior. Policy advisors, therefore, have had to rely on the ambiguous theoretical studies or on intuitive judgments" (Taylor 1993).

For this reason, in Taylor (1999a), I used an estimated multi-country model to calculate the quantitative impact on economic stability of a move from a flexible exchange rate between Germany, France, and Italy to a fixed exchange rate as in a single currency. The loss was there, but importantly not so large that it could not be offset by sound fiscal policy with automatic stabilizers.

For this approach to work, however, the new monetary policy had to be systematic and rule-like. In a paper, "What the European Central Bank Needs to Do" (Taylor 1999b), I argued that the ECB should follow a rules-based monetary policy so that a rules-based fiscal policy could be more easily constructed and followed.

However, as time went by and the years turned into decades, one could see actions and reactions which represented deviations from rules or strategies, and these have resulted in a move toward a more interventionist, less market-based institution. I will give empirical evidence of this move based on my research and that of others focusing on the years from 2003 to 2006 and from 2014 to 2018. To be sure, I am not referring to the famous "Whatever it takes" comments, but rather to specific monetary policy actions.

11.2 The Period Leading Up to the Global Financial Crisis: 2003–2006

That there were large deviations from rules-based policy in the years 2003–2006 leading up to the global financial crisis was shown empirically in research by Ahrend, Cournède, and Price at the Organisation for Economic Co-operation and Development (OECD 2008). Figures 11.1 and 11.2 summarize their results. The scatter plot in Fig. 11.1, which is drawn from their 2008 paper, shows, on the horizontal axis, the deviation from the Taylor rule in the eurozone countries. It was quite large for some

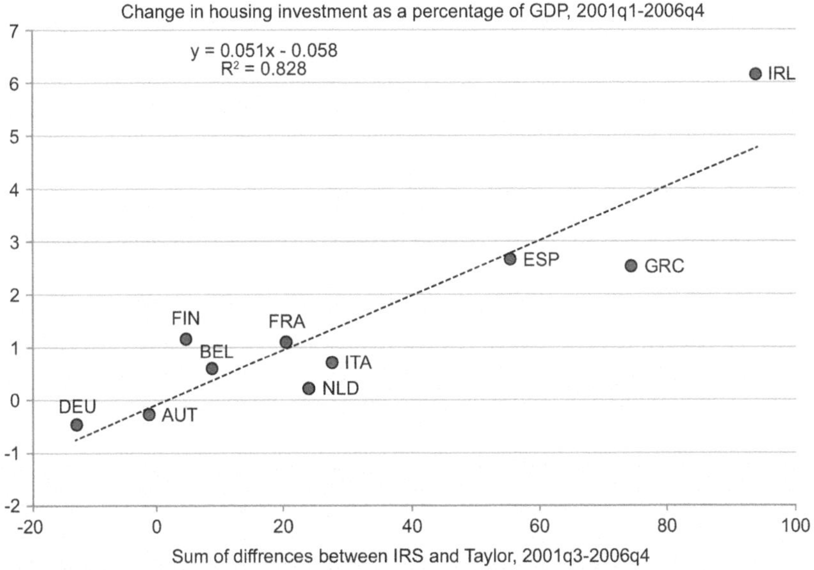

Fig. 11.1 ECB: Deviations from rules-based policy and housing investment. (*Source*: OECD 2008)

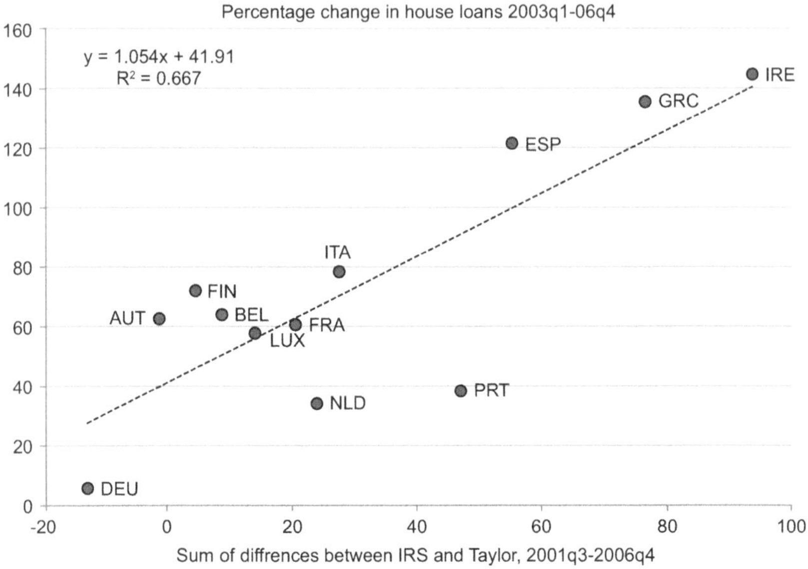

Fig. 11.2 ECB: Deviations from rules-based policy and housing loans. (*Source*: OECD 2008)

countries, especially Greece, Ireland, and Spain. Figure 11.1 also shows housing investment and thus the relationship between housing investment and the deviation from the rule. Figure 11.2 shows the relationship between housing *loans* and the same deviation over the same period.

Both Figs. 11.1 and 11.2 show a strong positive relationship between interest rate deviations from a rule-like policy and the housing market. The deviations are largest in Greece, Ireland, and Spain, and these are the three countries with the largest booms in both housing investment and lending according to the OECD data. According to Ahrend (2010, p. 19) "'below Taylor' episodes have generally been associated with the build-up of financial imbalances in housing markets."

Germany is on the other side of the scatter, with interest rates closer to the rule and much more modest developments in housing. Of course, within the eurozone, there is only one policy interest rate, but that rate was too low for macroeconomic conditions in some countries. Even within the "one-size-fits-all" framework of the eurozone, it appears that the rate could have been nearer the middle and thus higher. More recent evidence confirms this as I show later in this chapter.

Additional empirical research by Jordà et al. (2015) further examined the eurozone countries during this period, and it yielded similar results. They found that

> common monetary policy administered by the ECB meant that for some countries monetary conditions would be 'too loose,' whereas for some others they would be 'too tight.' Booming economies would be encouraged to grow, slumping economies to decline, resulting in greater real economic instability ... *Prima facie*, the events in the eurozone in the 1999–2008 pre-crisis phase seem to conform to this narrative. (Jordà et al. 2015, p. 9)

Figures 11.3, 11.4, and 11.5, featuring data from their paper, show their key findings. Figures compare three eurozone countries—Ireland, Spain, and Germany—over the period from 1999Q1 to 2008Q1. Figure 11.3 indicates that the ECB interest rate was too low for conditions in Ireland and Spain as measured by the Taylor rule throughout this period. In contrast, in Germany the interest rate was quite close, perhaps a bit on the high side, to what such a rule would say.

Figure 11.4 looks at mortgage lending as a share of GDP for these three countries. It shows that mortgage lending grew much more rapidly in Spain and Ireland compared with Germany, much as one would expect

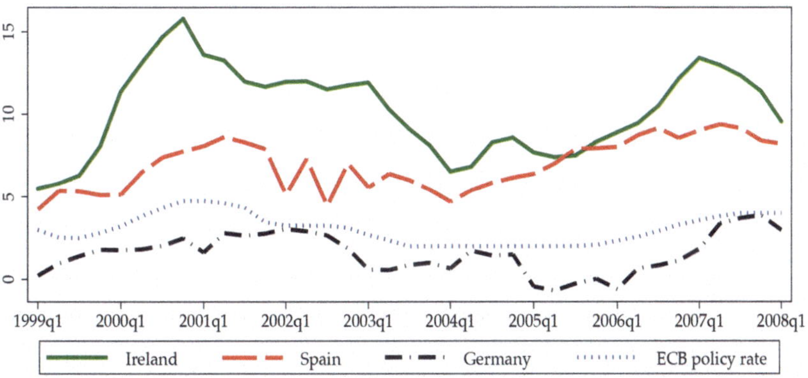

Fig. 11.3 ECB: Deviations from rules-based policy—Taylor rules and actual policy interest rates (% per year): Ireland, Spain, and Germany. (*Source*: Jordà et al. 2015, Fig. 6). (Color figure online)

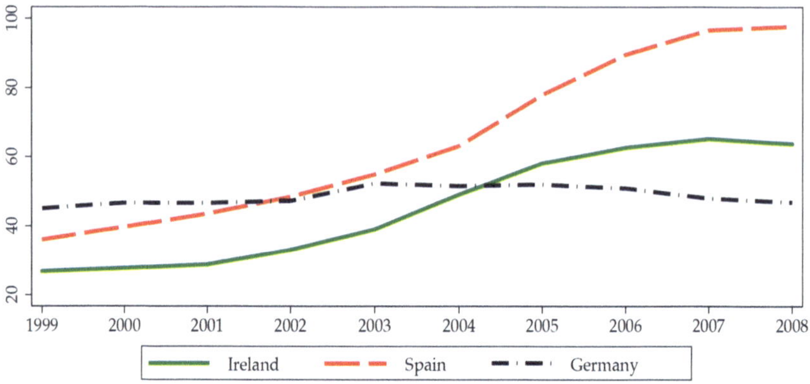

Fig. 11.4 ECB: Deviations from rules-based policy—mortgage lending to GDP ratio (%): Ireland, Spain, and Germany. (*Source*: Jordà et al. 2015, Fig. 6). (Color figure online)

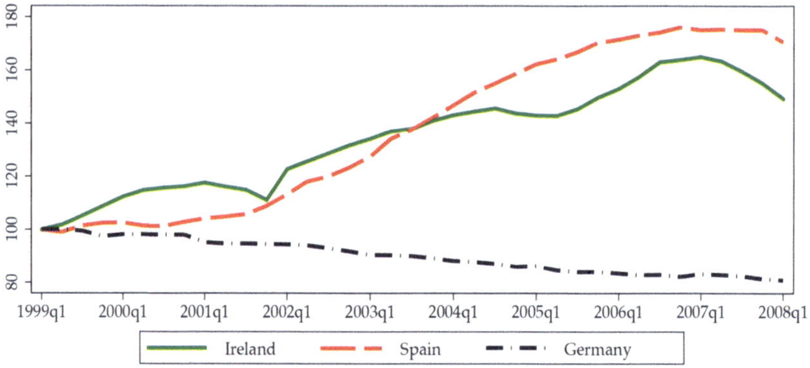

Fig. 11.5 ECB: Deviations from rules-based policy—house price to income ratio (1999Q1 = 100): Ireland, Spain, and Germany. (*Source*: Jordà et al. 2015, Fig. 6). (Color figure online)

from the interest rate difference. Figure 11.5 shows housing prices in the three countries, confirming the association of interest rate deviations from policy rules and housing price inflation pointed out by Ahrend et al. (2008). The authors write, "These data provide some support to the hypotheses, often asserted in analyses of the eurozone crisis, that periphery countries experienced an exogenous monetary easing which went on to fuel credit and housing price boom and bust cycles—ending in economic crises and output disasters for countries like Ireland and Spain."

More recent evidence comes from the *Annual Report* of the German Council of Economic Experts (2018). Figure 11.6, which is drawn from the *Report*, illustrates the findings. For four countries—Germany, France, Italy, and Spain—the charts in Fig. 11.6 show each country's policy rule and a range of interest rate settings around that rule. It also shows the actual interest rate of the ECB—the main refinancing rate—and a eurozone rule for the ECB.

As summarized by Wieland (2019), "Taylor rules for France, Germany, Italy and Spain suggest ECB policy too easy for Spain (a lot), Italy and France during boom years prior to financial crisis." In contrast the rate for Germany is close to what the policy rule for Germany would suggest. The

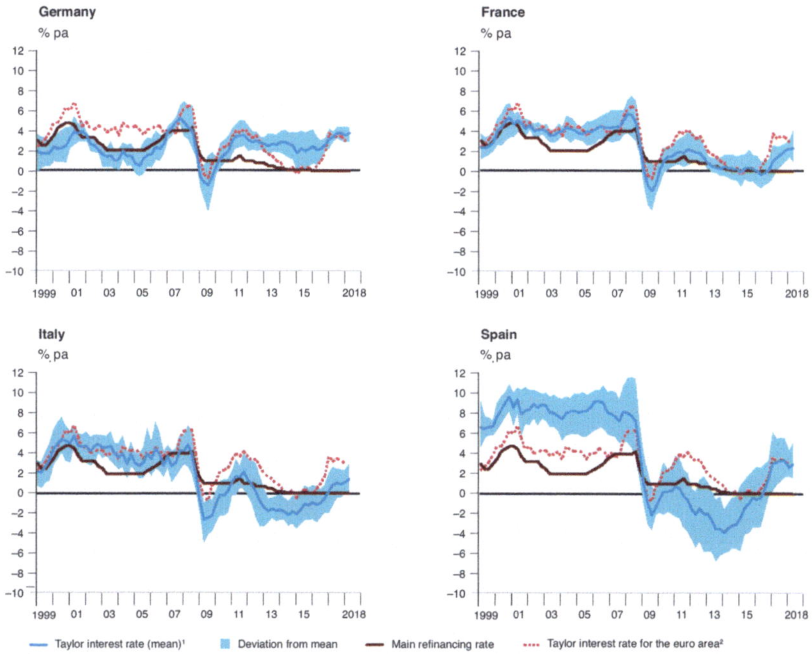

Fig. 11.6 ECB: Deviations from rules-based policy in four countries. (*Source*: 2018/19 Annual Report of the German Council of Economic Experts). (Color figure online)

Report confirms the findings of Ahrend, Cournède, and Price (OECD 2008) and Jordà et al. (2015), though it does not go on to consider the effects on housing.

One might ask, what caused these deviations? A possible explanation, which I favor, is that there is an international contagion of monetary policy actions from one central bank to another, including deviations from rules-based monetary policy. Other empirical results—some of which are contained in Ahrend, Cournède, and Price (OECD 2008) and Jordà et al. (2015)—show that there were deviations of interest rates from policy rules in other countries during the period running up to the crisis. The contagion is often due to exchange rate considerations.

Note that in Fig. 11.6 the policy rate for the ECB is somewhat lower than the policy rule for the whole ECB. Figure 11.7, presented at the European Central Bank Conference on "Globalisation and the Macroeconomy" in 2007 (Taylor 2007a), shows why this may have occurred. It indicates that there is a correlation between the Fed and the ECB. The blue line shows the deviation of the ECB policy rate from the Taylor rule

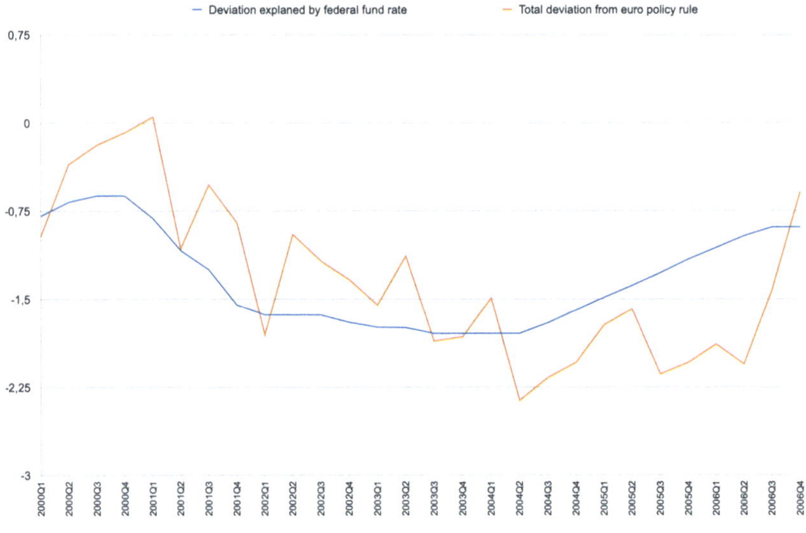

Fig. 11.7 Eurozone deviations from policy rule 2002–2005: a possible explanation. (*Source*: Taylor 2007a). (Color figure online)

with inflation measured as the four-quarter rate of change in the harmonized index of consumer prices.

A regression of this deviation on a constant and on the US federal funds rate shows a statistically significant coefficient on the federal funds rate of 0.21. The plot of the fitted values from this regression is shown by the red line in Fig. 11.7. Thus, a good part of negative residual (policy rate below the rule) at the ECB is "explained" by the federal funds rate being lower than normal. The connection illustrates the international contagion of monetary policy deviations.

There is, of course, much evidence that the federal funds rate was too low for too long in that period. Jarociński and Smets (2008), in research conducted at the ECB, found evidence of the Fed's "easy monetary policy" and that this policy "contributed to the boom in the housing market in 2004 and 2005." (See also Taylor 2007b.)

11.3 Large-Scale Asset Purchases and the Explosion of Reserve Balances: 2014–2018

To explore deviations from rules-based policy in more recent periods, we must recognize that the ECB has been using two separate monetary policy instruments in recent years: the policy interest rate and the size of the balance sheet. In Taylor (2019), I examined the balance sheet of the European Central Bank as well as the Federal Reserve and the Bank of Japan. The purchase of financial assets by these banks has been financed by increases in central bank liabilities, mainly "reserve balances." In addition, the ECB, and each of these other central banks, sets its short-term policy interest rate.

For the ECB and the two other central banks, the monetary policy framework thus includes six different policy instruments: the balance sheet items (R for reserve balances) R_E, R_U, and R_J, and the short-term policy rates (I for interest rate) I_E, I_U, I_J, where the subscripts indicate Europe (E), the United States (U), and Japan (J). Figure 11.8 shows the path of reserve balances in the ECB along with the exchange rate through January 2019. Note that there is a strong correlation between reserve balances and the exchange rate. In particular, the figure shows the weakening of the euro against the dollar after the large-scale expansion at the ECB.

Figure 11.9 shows the actual paths of reserve balances for the Fed and the Bank of Japan along with the ECB. The scale for reserve balances is

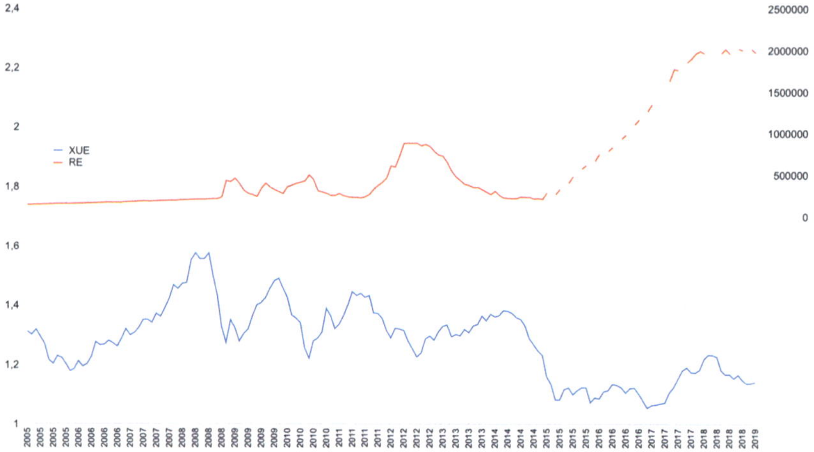

Fig. 11.8 Reserve balances (RE) at the ECB and euro-dollar exchange rate (XUE). (*Source*: Taylor 2019 (Updated)). (Color figure online)

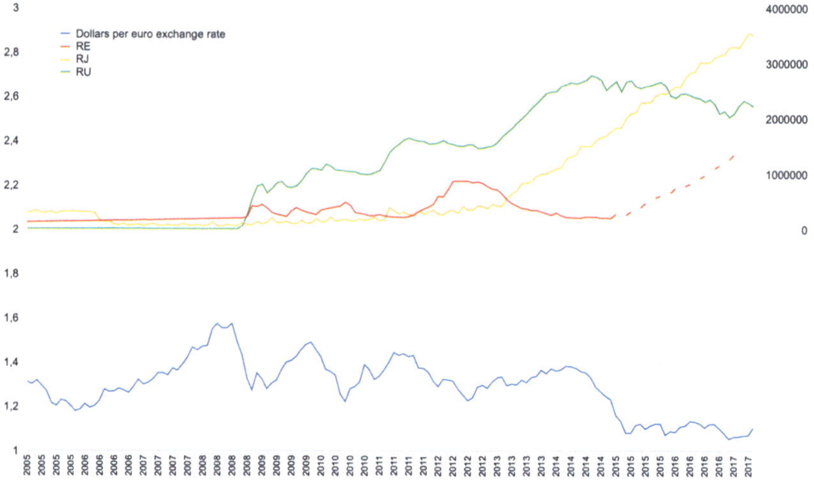

Fig. 11.9 Reserve balances at the ECB (RE), the Fed (RU), and the Bank of Japan (RJ). (*Source*: Taylor 2019). (Color figure online)

shown on the right-hand vertical axis measured in units of the local currency—millions of dollars, hundreds of million yen, and millions of euros. The lowest line in the figure is the exchange rate between the dollar and the euro.

The Fed started large-scale asset purchases of US Treasuries and mortgage-backed securities in 2009. These purchases, called quantitative easing (QE), were financed largely with reserve balances. This expansion of reserve balances in the United States was followed by an expansion by the Bank of Japan at the start of 2013. Soon thereafter, the ECB started increasing reserve balances. In other words, there is a positive correlation between reserve balances in these countries.

Various policy statements by central bankers are consistent with these time series: following the global financial crisis and the start of the US recovery, the yen significantly appreciated against the dollar as the Fed extended its large-scale asset purchase program financed with increases in reserve balances. The yen appreciation became a key issue in Japan. Lead by Haruhiko Kuroda, the Bank of Japan implemented its own quantitative easing, and a depreciation of the yen followed. The subsequent moves by the ECB toward quantitative easing were also due to concerns about an appreciating euro. At the Jackson Hole conference in August 2014, Mario Draghi spoke about these concerns and suggested quantitative easing, which soon followed. This shift in policy was followed by a weaker euro.

While the correlations show a close association between the policies in the different countries, there are also statistically significant exchange rate effects in estimated regressions of exchange rates on reserve balances, as reported in Taylor (2019). The regressions show that an increase in reserve balances by the ECB causes the euro to depreciate against the dollar. Similar effects are seen in other countries.

11.4 Conclusion

Looking back with perspective of the two decades since the euro and the ECB were created, one sees successes and developments that are consistent with the principles of economic freedom: the emphasis on transparency and clear communications about monetary policy, the very goal of price stability, the frequent endorsement of structural and market-based reforms in member countries, principle that automatic fiscal stabilizers and sound budget policy are key complementary parts of macroeconomic policy, the encouragement of open capital markets, and the notion, as expressed by Mario Draghi (2016), that "We would all clearly benefit from … improving communication over our reaction functions …."

These favorable developments contrast with actions that are less consistent with the principles of economic freedom and which are often observed in national institutions in Europe. One explanation for the developments is that many of these same ideas underlie the thinking of central bankers at many other central banks around the world and that central banks tend to follow each other as they endorse such ideas.

However, accompanying these favorable developments, as I see it, has been a deviation from rules-based policy and strategies, an increased use of discretionary interventions, and a resulting uncertainty about what the reaction function is. These interventions may have delayed the move to more classical liberal policies in other areas of economic policy.

These less-favorable developments have been rationalized by many factors, such as the effective lower bound on interest rates or changes in the transmission mechanism of monetary policy. But the research presented here shows that the actions and reactions relate more to international factors which have been a source of these deviations. Ironically, therefore, international influences and pressures that have led to policies more conducive to economic freedom may also have led to policies less conducive to economic freedom. If so, this is yet another reason for a rules-based reform of the international monetary system.

References

Ahrend, Rudiger. 2010. Monetary Ease: A Factor Behind Financial Crises? Some Evidence from OECD Countries. *Economics: An Open Access, Open Assessment e-journal* 4: 1–30. Accessed June 18, 2020. http://www.economics-ejournal.org/economics/journalarticles/2010-12.

Draghi, Mario. 2016. The International Dimension of Monetary Policy. Introductory Speech at The ECB Forum on Central Banking, Sintra, Portugal, June 28. Frankfurt am Main: ECB, DG Communications. Accessed June 18, 2020. https://www.ecb.europa.eu/press/key/date/2016/html/sp160628.en.html.

German Council of Economic Experts. 2018. Vor wichtigen wirtschaftspolitischen Weichenstellungen—Setting the Right Course for Economic Policy. In *Jahresgutachten—Annual Report 2018/19*, ed. Sachverständigenrat zur Begutachtung der gesamtwirtschaftlichen Entwicklung, 1–78. Wiesbaden: Statistisches Bundesamt (Destatis). Accessed June 3, 2020. https://www.

sachverstaendigenrat-wirtschaft.de/fileadmin/dateiablage/gutachten/jg201819/JG2018-19_gesamt.pdf.

Issing, Otmar. 2014. Communications and Transparency—The Example of the ECB. *Journal of Economic Dynamics and Control* 49: 70–73. Accessed June 18, 2020. https://EconPapers.repec.org/RePEc:eee:dyncon:v:49:y:2014:i:c:p:70-73.

Jarociński, Marek, and Frank R. Smets. 2008. House Prices and the Stance of Monetary Policy. ECB Working Paper Series 891: 1–49. Frankfurt am Main, Germany: European Central Bank. Accessed June 18, 2020. https://www.ecb.europa.eu/pub/pdf/scpwps/ecbwp891.pdf.

Jordà, Òscar, Moritz Schularick, and Alan M. Taylor. 2015. Betting the House. *Journal of International Economics* 96: 2–18. Accessed June 18, 2020. https://EconPapers.repec.org/RePEc:eee:inecon:v:96:y:2015:i:s1:p:s2-s18.

OECD, Rudiger Ahrend, Boris Cournède, and Robert Price. 2008. Monetary Policy, Market Excesses and Financial Turmoil. *OECD Economics Department Working Papers* 597: 1–39. Accessed June 3, 2020. https://www.oecd-ilibrary.org/economics/monetary-policy-market-excesses-and-financial-turmoil_244200148201.

Taylor, John B. 1993. *Macroeconomic Policy in a World Economy.* New York: W.W. Norton.

———. 1999a. The Robustness and Efficiency of Monetary Policy Rules as Guidelines for Interest Rate Setting by the European Central Bank. *Journal of Monetary Economics* 43: 655–679. Accessed June 18, 2020. https://EconPapers.repec.org/RePEc:eee:moneco:v:43:y:1999:i:3:p:655-679.

———. 1999b. What the European Central Bank Needs to Do. *Hoover Digest* 1: 92–95. Accessed June 18, 2020. https://www.hoover.org/research/what-european-central-bank-needs-do.

———. 2007a. Monetary Policy in a Global Economy: Past and Future Research Challenges. Written Version of the Keynote Address Presented at the ECB Conference on Globalisation and the Macroeconomy, Frankfurt am Mein, Germany, July 24.

———. 2007b. Housing and Monetary Policy. In *Housing, Housing Finance, and Monetary Policy*, ed. Jackson Hole, 463–476. Wyoming: Federal Reserve Bank of Kansas City.

———. 2019. *Reform of the International Monetary System: Why and How?* Cambridge, MA: MIT Press.

Wieland, Volker. 2019. Twitter Status. Last modified February 26. Accessed June 17, 2020. https://twitter.com/WielandVolker/status/1100349880248217600/photo/1.

CHAPTER 12

Dealing with the Covid Debt Overhang

Agnès Bénassy-Quéré and Francesco Giavazzi

Economic forecasting is famous for being extremely difficult. In times of COVID, the economic outlook crucially depends on the evolution of the pandemic and on the eventual development and deployment of a vaccine. The best that economic forecasters can do is to draw scenarios.

According to a not too unlikely scenario, a vaccine could be available in 2021. After the vast majority of the population has been vaccinated, the pandemic would disappear. According to one view, assuming COVID-19 is not replaced by COVID-20 or any COVID-20s, life would recover very much like pre-crisis: after all, the dramatic terrorist attacks of the last two decades did not have long-lasting effects. People are eager to enjoy their lives. And even with lower GDP Europe will remain a relatively prosperous region in the world.

A. Bénassy-Quéré
Université Paris 1 Panthéon Sorbonne, Paris, France
e-mail: agnes.benassy@univ-paris1.fr

F. Giavazzi (✉)
IGIER, Bocconi University, Milan, Italy
e-mail: francesco.giavazzi@unibocconi.it

F. Giavazzi et al. (eds.), *The Liberal Heart of Europe*,
https://doi.org/10.1007/978-3-030-60368-7_12

An alternative view suggests that the experience of the long lockdown could have changed habits and priorities with significant effects on industrial structure. Just think about university teaching, which is unlikely to abandon at least some online teaching, or business travel, most of which has been proven useless. How long-lasting the effects of the 2020 pandemic will be on consumer habits will determine the shape of the recession and its legacy.

12.1 V-Shaped or a Swoosh?

What will the post-COVID-19 recovery look like? "V-shaped" or "Swoosh-shaped"? This is a crucial question: for companies that are rewriting their investment plans for the coming years and for governments and central banks that are calibrating the economic policy that will accompany the recovery.

Here again there are two different views among economists. Larry Summers (2020) leans toward the V-shape. At the end of 2020, he said, we will remember the pandemic just as, at Christmas 2001, we remembered September 11: we had already forgotten about it. Paul Krugman (2020) also thinks along these lines.

On the opposite side, Barrero et al. (2020) think that the recovery will be slow because it will require a large reallocation of capital and labor: from sectors that after COVID will disappear to sectors that instead will enjoy a boom. These reallocations take time: trying to accelerate the recovery would mean preventing them, at a very high cost—we would have wasted COVID's opportunity. Understanding who is right has huge implications for businesses and economic policy actors alike. Betting on the wrong outcome would mean, for a company, either prolonging an unsustainable situation or missing an unrepeatable opportunity. The same applies to economic policy actors. Who is right?

Pagano et al. (2020) analyze option prices and find evidence in favor of a slow recovery. Looking back, and checking for traditional risk premium measures, the chapter documents that already before COVID-19, the US stock market was rewarding companies with a business model more compatible with social distancing, suggesting an awareness of pandemic risk well in advance of the outbreak of 2020. Looking ahead—and using option prices in the U.S. stock market up to the end of April 2020 to measure market expectations after the pandemic began—they find that this continues to be true after the first COVID outbreak. Over a two-year time horizon, investors expect the shares of the most pandemic-resistant companies to produce significantly lower returns than the least resistant: their relatively low expected returns are the price to pay for lower exposure to catastrophic risk. These differences are enormous in the case of some companies. For example, in early April 2020, the expected returns on the stocks of low-resilience companies such as Royal Caribbean and United Airlines were around 60% and 40%, respectively, while those of high resilience companies, such as Apple and Microsoft, were between 3% and 4%. In other words, the market prices of some companies are extraordinarily low because investors, perhaps thinking of pandemics, consider them exposed to a very high risk.

What does this have to do with the speed of recovery and its legacy? The market prices of companies are giving investors the signal to focus on the most resilient companies and stay away from the less resilient ones. The market is giving the signal that, for example, cruises on ships with thousands of passengers crammed on the decks are unlikely to have a future in their present business model. Ditto possibly for airlines. On the other hand, the share price of Zoom has doubled in less than six months because registrations to the platform have exploded. Distinguishing zombies from potential success stories, however, will be difficult. And, of course, the market may be wrong.

So what? "V-shaped" or "Swoosh-shaped"? If the recovery will be accompanied by a profound reallocation of production, and therefore of labor and capital, this will take time, certainly much longer than the alternative of returning to a world as we knew it until last year. A slower recovery then, but one that would take us into a more resilient world. Governments, if they defend non-resilient companies, for example, by keeping afloat cruise companies whose future depends on their ability to reinvent themselves, are hindering the transition to a more resilient world.

12.2 Debt: The Legacy of the Pandemic

What will be the legacy of the crisis in Europe? Even a fast recovery would legate a huge amount of public and private debts, both due to the dramatic months of shutdowns. A slow recovery would inflate these debts, the more so if capital and labor need to be massively reallocated. Also, a prolonged period of high unemployment and an increase in income and social inequalities may result in long-lasting disruptions in our already fragile societies. From the Global Financial Crisis (GFC), we know that social and political crises tend to lag behind economic disruptions. Here, we concentrate on the debt legacy.

During the lockdowns, firms have been offered loans, tax deferrals, tax cuts and short-time employment arrangements. They will re-emerge with higher debts vis-à-vis tax authorities, banks and markets. On their side, governments have largely acted as insurers for the private sector. Sovereign debts will jump by (at least) 15–25% of GDP in 2020, according to the European Commission's Spring forecasts.

In contrast, European households, on average, have been compensated during the lockdowns while being unable to spend their income. Hence, they have accumulated savings (Fig. 12.1). How they will use these savings is one of the big unknowns of the recovery. They could:

- Spend on consumption or investment, which would support the recovery;

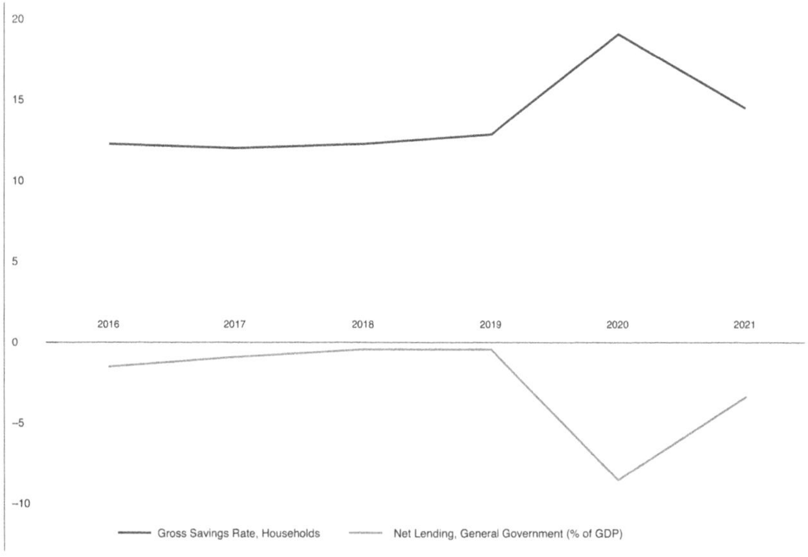

Fig. 12.1 Households' savings and government deficit, euro area. (*Source*: European Commission's Spring forecasts 2020)

- Lend to governments and (indirectly) to firms, which would contribute to keeping interest rates at a low level and to limit the collapse of investment;
- Invest in equity, which would contribute to repairing corporate balance sheets and help those that need to change their business model;
- Be asked to pay higher taxes, which would help governments cope with additional costs but with a negative impact on the recovery (see the experience of the GFC's aftermaths).

Although the COVID crisis has translated into a mixture of supply and demand shocks, the net effect so far has been deflationary; hence the readiness of the European Central Bank (ECB) to increase its purchases of sovereign debts. Assuming that the Pandemic Emergency Purchase Program (PEPP) will be carried out as planned, governments will be able to issue more debt at constant, very low interest rates. Hence, it will be crucial to channel private savings to private consumption and investment.

Incentivizing households to spend will not be easy until the situation has stabilized on both health and employment fronts. Hence (1) governments will have again to spend more in order to restart the economy, and (2) it will be crucial to find a way to channel part of households' savings to corporate equity while (possibly) limiting the risk for the households.

This issue so far has not been much debated. What we wrote earlier about the uncertainty in separating resilient from non-resilient firms suggests that equity investment could be risky: the possibility of betting on zombie firms is high. In this area, governance will be key and the presence of government-sponsored equity could be risky since governments tend to be biased toward defending jobs, as opposed to defending workers who might need to find a new job. Good governance should guarantee the correct division of labor: governments should concentrate on protecting workers hit by reallocations. Independent managers should be entrusted with the choice of surviving firms, trying to avoid creating a mass of zombie firms.

12.3 Dealing with the Pandemic Legacy Debt

After zombie firms has been dealt with, the balance sheets of surviving firms repaired and the economy restarted, in a scenario of no major new pandemic outbreak until a vaccine is introduced, EU member states will be left with a legacy of sovereign debts. Most of these debts will be national sovereign debts, the remainder being issued by the European Union (EU) according to the program (Next Generation EU, or NG-EU) proposed by the Commission. (Some debts are also to be issued at EU or euro area level on behalf of individual member states, through the SURE program and the European Stability Mechanism pandemic credit line.) For a while, a large part of this debt will be kept in the balance sheet of the ECB. But what to do over the medium term?

In thinking about this issue, it is important to keep the pandemic legacy debt issued since the Spring of 2020 separate from the debt inherited from the past. Only the former arises from the response to a common shock. This distinction is important because many proposals have been tabled to address the debt inherited from the past. This debt, however, is the result of country-specific shocks and country-specific policy responses to such shocks. Dealing with it by avoiding some form of mutualization is difficult and, in any case, it is a very different problem (see Vihriälä 2020).

So, let us consider pandemic legacy debt (see also Soros 2020). The optimal way to deal with a shock such as the COVID-induced pandemic is to spread its cost onto future generations, in a similar way as after a war. There are different ways of doing this. The first one is through the issuance of perpetual bonds, that is, debts that will never be repaid and pay a fixed coupon forever. As argued by Giavazzi and Tabellini (2020), this solution is safe since the government only needs to pay the interest and never faces rollover risk. The problem with this first solution is that such "consols" would probably have to offer a relatively high interest rate in order to compensate investors for the duration risk (see Corsetti et al. 2020). A second possibility to deal with the cost of the COVID crisis is through the issuance of standard, redeemable debts to be rolled over indefinitely or over a very long period. Depending on the maturity of the debts issued, this second avenue will create rollover risks, but it will benefit from current very low interest rates.

The trade-off between the cost of the debt and the rollover risk could be overcome if an institution committed to buy these bonds and roll them over indefinitely. It has been suggested that the ECB could play this role. However, keeping an inflating balance sheet forever would reduce the ability of the ECB to control a possible resurgence of inflation. To avoid this, the ECB could sterilize its bond holdings by issuing central bank bonds (and destroying central bank money). The question is whether the ECB is the right place to transform risky assets into safe assets. As argued by Pâris and Wyplosz (2014), another institution such as the European Stability Mechanism could play this role as long as its own borrowings are backed by a safe, common revenue (Pâris and Wyplosz suggest that the member states waive their seigniorage revenues which would then pay the interests on the common debts).

The Commission's proposal to finance its NG-EU plan goes in this direction: the plan is to borrow by issuing EU bonds at relatively long maturities in order to finance targeted investments in the member states and to back the borrowing at least partially by own resources. The fact that the program will be temporary does not necessarily involve that the debts will have to be repaid. They could be rolled over at little risk if backed by a common, permanent revenue stream. It could even be argued that these common debts should not be repaid for the sake of financial stability: the banking sector would be more stable if it could hold more EU, "safe" assets and less national debts the value of which may diverge in periods of financial stress.

What about the debt issued by individual member states since the start of the pandemic? So far, they have largely been purchased by the ECB: by the end of the year 2020 the ECB's PEPP program will have bought roughly 1.35 trillion-euro worth of bonds (11.3% of eurozone GDP), mostly sovereign bonds issued by eurozone states. The ECB has announced its willingness to roll over maturing bonds until inflation recovers solidly toward the "close to 2%" objective. Hence, as long as inflation remains at a low level, these debts will be rolled over.

What if inflationary pressures arise? If inflation comes along with a resumption of growth in the euro area, then debt sustainability will be less of a concern, and reducing the ECB's holdings will not be too difficult. In a stagflation scenario, though, the ECB would be in a very difficult position. This is where a Politically Acceptable Debt Restructuring in the Eurozone (PADRE)-like permanent debt exchange system would be helpful.

12.4 Conclusions

The recovery from the dramatic COVID crisis is still full of unknowns. What is sure, though, is that national governments will emerge from the crisis with a new pile of debts. The latter will be benign as long as interest rates remain close to zero (or if the recovery is strong enough for GDP growth to exceed the interest rate) and if there is stable demand for these debts even at very low rates. Central banks will undoubtedly play a key role. In the euro area, the challenge is to consolidate the fiscal and political institutions so as the ECB can be stabilizing while acting within its mandate. The "Next Generation" plan of the European Commission can be understood as a major step in this direction.

References

Barrero, Jose Maria, Nicholas Bloom, and Steven J. Davis. 2020. Covid-19 Is Also a Reallocation Shock. NBER Working Paper, 27137. Cambridge, MA: National Bureau of Economic Research.

Corsetti, Giancarlo, Aitor Erce, and Antonio Garcia-Pascual. 2020. Perpetual Bonds Are Not the Best Way to Finance the European Recovery Fund. *VoxEU*, May 14. Accessed June 9, 2020. https://voxeu.org/article/using-perpetual-bonds-finance-european-recovery-fund.

Giavazzi, Francesco, and Guido Tabellini. 2020. Covid Perpetual Eurobonds: Jointly Guaranteed and Supported by the ECB. *VoxEU*, March 24. Accessed June 9, 2020. https://voxeu.org/article/covid-perpetual-eurobonds.

Krugman, Paul. 2020. The Audacity of Slope: How Fast a Recovery? Web Seminar Held in 'The Economic Implications of COVID-19' Series at the Princeton Bendheim Center for Finance, Princeton, New Jersey, May 15. Accessed June 9, 2020. Published on YouTube on May 16. https://youtu.be/h1ZiTIou0_8.

Pagano, Marco, Christian Wagner, and Josef Zechner. 2020. Disaster Resilience and Asset Prices. CSEF Working Papers, 563. Naples: Centre for Studies in Economics and Finance (CSEF), University of Naples.

Pâris, Pierre, and Charles Wyplosz. 2014. *PADRE: Politically Acceptable Debt Restructuring in the Eurozone*. Geneva Reports on the World Economy, Special Report 3. Geneva: International Center for Monetary and Banking Studies.

Soros, George. 2020. The EU Should Issue Perpetual Bonds. *Project Syndicate*, May 25. Accessed June 9, 2020. https://www.project-syndicate.org/commentary/perpetual-bonds-are-essential-to-european-union-survival-by-george-soros-2020-05.

Summers, Larry. 2020. COVID-19 and the Global Economy. Web Seminar Held in 'The Economic Implications of COVID-19' Series at the Princeton Bendheim Center for Finance, Princeton, New Jersey, May 22. Published on YouTube on May 22. Accessed June 9, 2020. https://youtu.be/cZmRtQCR2ns.

Vihriälä, Vesa. 2020. Make room for fiscal action through debt conversion, Vox-EU, April 15, 2020.

CHAPTER 13

Globalization and Its Critics

Leszek H. Balcerowicz

There is a massive literature on globalization (e.g. see Bordo 2017). Therefore, I limit my comments on this fundamentally important process to a bare minimum (Sect. 13.1). Instead, I focus on the criticisms of globalization. Section 13.2 distinguishes three points of view of this process: economic, political economy, and moral. In Sect. 13.3 I briefly discuss crude anti-globalism of the nationalistic and utopian variety. Then I move to more sophisticated versions of the discussions of globalizations focusing on what I perceive to be lack of clarity, misconceptions, or outright fallacies. Section 13.4 deals with trade globalization and Sect. 13.5 with financial globalization. In Sect. 13.6, I formulate some final observations and recommendations.

13.1 Globalization and Its Components

In the most general sense, the process of globalization consists in increasing contacts (including contracts) among individuals and organizations from various countries. In this sense it is the opposite of isolationism.

L. H. Balcerowicz (✉)
Warsaw School of Economics, Warsaw, Poland
e-mail: lbalce@sgh.waw.pl

F. Giavazzi et al. (eds.), *The Liberal Heart of Europe*,
https://doi.org/10.1007/978-3-030-60368-7_13

Economic globalization is reflected in the growing integration of markets (Bordo 2017). In each period there is a level (state) of globalization as measured by various ratios, for example, world exports to global GDP or the migrant population to the world population. Globalization is usually divided into:

- Trade globalization, that is, trade in material products;
- Financial globalization, that is, flows of capital;
- International migration.

One should add globalization of communication, that is, increased flow of data which distinguishes modern globalization, with the invention of the telegraph and later information and communications technology (ICT), from the whole history of mankind until the nineteenth century. An interesting question is to what extent can this technology replace face-to-face contacts between people from various places (Baldwin 2016).

Another addition is the globalization of services, that is, goods, the production of which cannot be separated from their consumption. Therefore, the globalization of services has to be contained (until recently) in other flows:

- Many services are contained in the goods which are moved across borders.
- Foreign direct investment (FDI), that is, part of financial globalization, creates firms in foreign countries which offer services for business (e.g. consulting or accounting) or for consumers, for example, McDonald's.
- Consumers of services move to foreign countries (international tourism).
- Providers of certain services, for example, construction workers, move to another country for a certain period of time.
- Modern improvements in ICTs enable the growth of tele-services, whereby a producer (e.g. a surgeon) performs the services at a distance. Therefore, ICT allows the spatial separation of production and consumption.

Finally, it is useful to see which components of globalization are most closely related to technology transfer, which is the most important driver in closing the gap between the less and more developed countries. Massive empirical research indicates that this role is played in particular by exports and imports of manufactured products, by the immigration of skilled people, and by the FDI, as opposed to "pure" financial flows, especially those that finance increased government spending or the housing booms.

Therefore, in analyzing the growth prospects for the respective countries one should consider not only the overall scale but also the composition of the globalization flows they receive. But remember that the scale and composition of those flows depend on the institutional systems and policies of the receiving countries.

13.2 Three Points of View on Globalization

Globalization is analyzed and assessed from three points of view: (1) economic, (2) political economy, and (3) moral (ethical).

The economic analysis aims in general to explain the socioeconomic outcomes, for example, growth, stability, poverty, (un)employment, and inequalities. This is also its main task with reference to globalization. Massive economic research has shown that trade isolationism, present in the socialist (non-market) economies and in the distorted, quasi-statist market economies, has been very costly in terms of foregone economic growth and thus lower standard of living of millions of people (O'Rourke et al. 1996; Wolf 2004). One should remember that many professional economists had advocated socialism, that is, the replacement of private ownership by the monopoly of state ownership and the replacement of the market by central planning (Balcerowicz 1995). It should not be forgotten that the statist doctrine of import substitution was until recently a part of mainstream economics, and it was supported by the World Bank (Wolf 2004). The present discussion on the economics of trade globalization also often suffers from the lack of clarity, wrong assessments, and sometimes wrong recommendations. I will come to this issue in Sects. 13.3, 13.4, and 13.5.

The political economy analysis aims at explaining political outcomes by linking them to various more or less probable causes, including socioeconomic outcomes. One should be very careful in drawing general conclusions from specific cases, for example, from the present political backlash against trade globalization in the US under the then candidate and now former President Trump. I think that political outcomes are probably more difficult to explain than economic ones because of a larger role of chance factors (including the appearance of special individuals) in the former case than in the latter. Besides, even if one can convincingly link the anti-globalist political outcomes to import competition (and that is a *big* "if"—see later), there remains a basic question: what would be the policy recommendations?

The moral analysis should not be confused with moralizing. The moral analysis deals with the moral standards of judging various outcomes, including those that are—rightly or wrongly—linked to globalization. All too often economists—and even more other social scientists—focus on the people whom they regard as globalization's "losers" in developed economies and disregard the beneficiaries of globalization in poor countries (not to mention the winners in the developed states). Such a focus is a display *of nationalistic ethics.*

Universal ethics, on the contrary, considers the consequences of globalization for all groups in the world and especially for the poor. And the gains for the latter from the reforms which have opened the way to globalization have been huge. As Fig. 13.1 shows, the poor gained the most from trade as their consumption patterns are focused on tradable goods, for example, food and manufactured goods, and to lesser extent services: in moving away from autarky to trade, the relative prices of goods consumed by the poor, such as food, fall more. The gains from opening to trade are estimated at 63% for the 10th percentile of the income distribution and 28% for the 90th percentile. The poor gain the most in each of the 40 countries modeled: the sample for Fig. 13.1 consists of 27 EU member states, Turkey, the US, Canada, Brazil, Japan, Korea, Taiwan, China, India, and Indonesia.

As can also be seen in Fig. 13.2, in 1981, 42% of the world population lived at $1.90 (2011 USD, PPP) and only 11% in 2013. This is despite the fact that world population increased during this time by 59%.

Finally, there is a *utopian* ethics which demands that people be guided by altruism in their mutual interactions and condemns markets, including the global ones, because they rely on the self-interest of the buyers and sellers. Needless to say, it is a display of irrationality, of deep ignorance about evolutionary psychology and history, and it is an offense against common sense.

It is interesting to note that the proponents of nationalistic and utopian ethics share the same slogans. For example, they criticize free trade in the name of "fair trade"—even though they give various meanings to this expression.

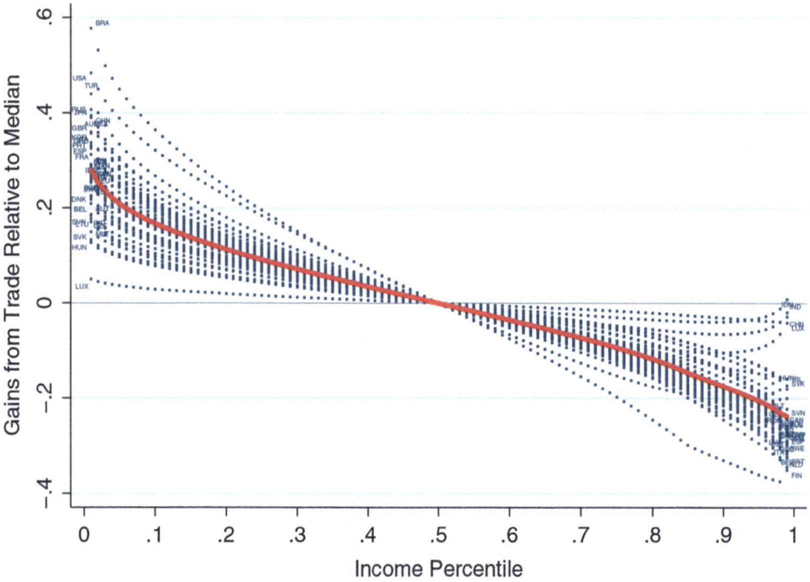

Fig. 13.1 Distribution of unequal gains from trade—deviations are relative to the median individual; solid line is the average. (*Source*: Fajgelbaum and Khandelwal 2016, Fig. 5). (Color figure online)

Fig. 13.2 World population in poverty and not. (*Source*: World Bank). (Color figure online)

I know very well that the nationalistic ethics is much stronger in politics than the universal one. But this is not an argument in favor of the academics who strengthen this bias by bashing globalization in the name of defending globalization's "losers" in rich countries and who disregard its beneficiaries in the poor ones. At the minimum, they should not pretend to represent a moral high ground, and they should not be regarded as such by other people.

13.3 Crude Anti-globalism

Crude anti-globalism appears in two forms: the anti-capitalist propaganda, based on utopian ethics and on a complete disregard of economic history and of analytical economics—it usually appears under the label of the "left"—and the nationalistic propaganda, which is based on nationalistic ethics and targets foreigners as migrants or producers of imported goods, and usually belongs to the "right."

The main representatives of the crude anti-globalism stem from outside mainstream economics, even though some professional economists lend credibility to this phenomenon by focusing on those who are considered the losers in the developed world and on the inequalities ascribed to trade globalization.

Martin Wolf (2004) has brilliantly exposed the logical and empirical fallacies of crude anti-globalism. The main ones include the following: (1) propositions to replace the globalized world with one consisting of many self-sufficient units; (2) advocating replacing capitalism with "something nicer"; (3) claiming that globalization destroys national states and democracy: (4) demonizing multinational corporations; (5) claiming that globalization is responsible for mass destitution by fostering increased inequality within and between nations; (6) blaming globalization for the destruction of the environment, and the like.

I will now deal with more sophisticated versions of anti-globalism (which sometimes border the crude form). However, I would like to stress that crude anti-globalism, with its false simplicity and emotionally loaded accusations, is a dangerous phenomenon which, for those very reasons, enjoys mass popularity. In that, it resembles the previous quasi-religious or nationalistic movements: Communism and Fascism. Therefore, the proponents of reason and of a liberal order should unmask the fallacies of crude anti-globalization in the mass media, as the propaganda which does not meet a strong response tends to win.

13.4 Trade Globalization

In discussing trade globalization, one should consider two types of institutions and policies (for short: policies): those which determine the scope of a country's openness to trade (Policy 1) and those which influence the individuals' possibilities and incentives to adjust to new opportunities and threats, including changes that are linked to trade opening (Policy 2). Socioeconomic outcomes result from various factors. One of the analytical challenges is to isolate the impact of trade opening from that of other factors, especially of technological change (Autor et al. 2015) which, in turn, depends on countries' institutional systems: there is no good substitute for extensive and equal economic freedom within the framework of the rule of law.

Socioeconomic outcomes influence politics even though there are many other factors. Figure 13.3 depicts these and other interactions. I will use it to discuss the impact of globalization on the less developed countries first and then on rich economies.

In speaking about trade globalization, one must consider the demise of socialism, first in China and later in the former Soviet bloc. This has opened the way to the market reforms in these countries, including the liberalization of trade (Fig. 13.2). There can be little doubt that these liberal reforms were hugely beneficial to societies in the former socialist

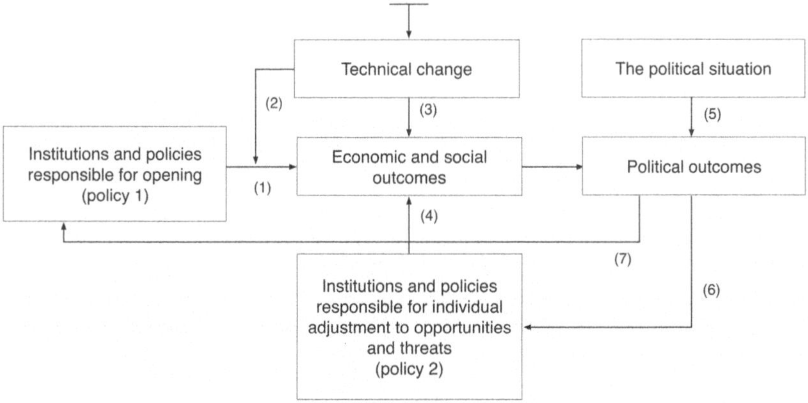

Fig. 13.3 Policies, globalization, outcomes

countries. For counterexamples, look to North Korea, Cuba, and Venezuela (Fig. 13.4).

The increase of exports (and imports) of the post-socialist economies depended not only on their radical institutional change but also on the appearance and spread of ICT-based products and services, invented in the developed countries. This technology has allowed a rapid development of global value chains (Baldwin 2016). This is an example of the interaction between radical institutional change in former socialist economies and modern technology stemming from the West in driving trade globalization. The largest beneficiaries on the exporting side have been, of course, China and, in Europe, Poland. Russia has increased its dependence on the production and exports of oil and gas.

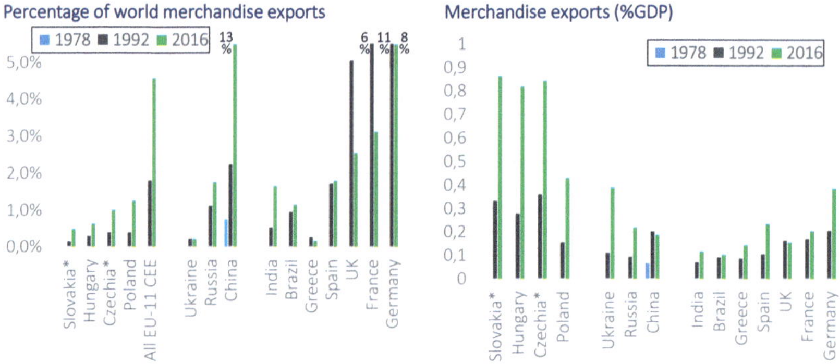

Fig. 13.4 Exports of post-communist economies pre- and post-transition and selected other exporters. (*Source*: own calculation; UNCTAD; FRED (only for current 2009 USD conversion). *For Czechia and Slovakia the year is 1993 instead of 1992 due to the dissolution of Czechoslovakia. Note 1: "All EU-11 CEE" stands for all 11 EU post-Communist economies. These have high GDP export shares as they are mostly small open economies, and exports are high within the EU. Note 2: Declines in world export share of the UK, France, and Germany are in line with a general decline in export shares of high-income economies from 84% in 1992 to 67% in 2016. Note 3: Russian exports increased, but they are mostly composed of raw materials. UN COMTRADE database shows that the share of minerals, metals, vegetables, foodstuffs, and wood in Russian export stood at 81% in 2016 (63% in 1995). According to the Harvard Atlas of Economic Complexity the diversity and ubiquity of Russian exports between 1995 and 2016 has fallen. (Color figure online)

The socioeconomic outcomes in poor globalizing countries depended not only on the scope of their trade opening (Policy 1) but also on their Policy 2, which determines the extent to which resources move in response to trade liberalization.

Here it is interesting to compare China and India (Fig. 13.5). As one can see, the structural shift from agriculture to manufacturing (proxied by the increase of urbanization) has been much larger in China than in India. The difference is mostly due to the fact that India has had much stronger barriers to spatial and occupational mobility: poor infrastructure, poor education, heavy subsidization of agriculture, and very restrictive labor laws which discouraged private firms from hiring new people (Kazmin 2014). This is an example of how bad Policy 2 limits the gains from trade globalization for the poor. Urbanization has been much larger in China, contributing to better economic performance.

I will now move to political outcomes which one can link to the opening of the economy in the poorer countries. It appears to me that there have been very few protests against the results of this systemic institutional change, either in China or in Eastern Europe. This is in contrast to anti-globalization protests in the rich countries.

Let me now use Fig. 13.3 to discuss the socioeconomic outcomes and political reactions to trade globalization in developed countries. In this

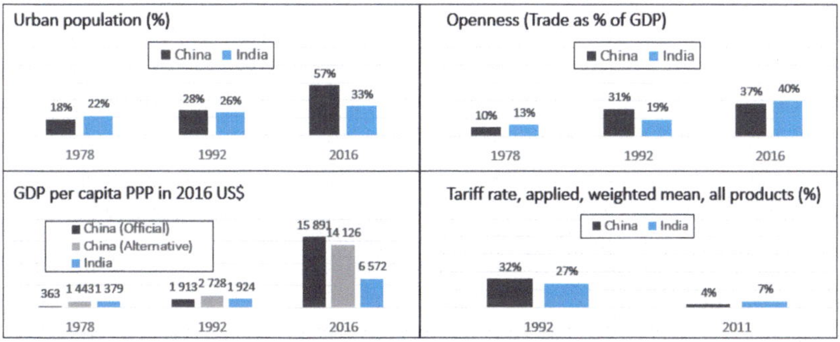

Fig. 13.5 Urbanization and economic performance in China and India. (*Source*: World Bank for urban population, openness, and tariffs; Total Database (May 2017) for GDP statistics. Note: The accuracy of official Chinese GDP data is disputed; therefore, we show both official and alternative figures. Alternative data has been calculated from Harry X. Wu and the Conference Board China Center 2014). (Color figure online)

case, Policies 1 refer to the trade liberalization and other market reforms in poorer economies, and the trade agreements concluded between them and the rich economies, for example, North American Free Trade Agreement. Policies 2 and outcomes in Fig. 13.1 refer to the developed countries.

What strikes me is that the popular and academic discussions about the outcomes linked, rightly or wrongly, to trade globalization are recently dominated by the negative issues (messages), especially regarding the increase in income inequalities and the related topic of the globalization's "losers." This seems to be truer for the US than for Europe, where the negative news focuses more on immigration. There are two main issues related to trade globalization in the developed economies: (1) the role of import competition and technological change in producing outcomes criticized as negative by some observers and politicians and, more importantly, (2) the role of policies which determine the individuals' adjustment (Policy 2).

The relative role of import competition versus ICT-related technological change is subject to intensive empirical research. Without going deeper into this literature, I would like to note that job losses occur in the non-tradable sector, too, and therefore, they cannot be ascribed to import competition, for example, Uber, or automation of clerical functions. And much of the increased imports from less developed countries include intra-industry trade within the expanded global value chains, made possible by the ICT and IT technology, developed in the rich countries (Baldwin 2016). Therefore, the increased import competition results from the interaction of the market reforms in the less developed countries, especially China, and modern technology from the rich countries. These developments, as I already mentioned, have provided enormous benefits to the poor in the poorer part of the world (and to many people in the richer part of our globe). But, in the West, the popular discussions and the political debates focus on globalization's "losers" and on inequalities within the rich economies.

However, it is not most important that the popular focus on the "losers" and on inequalities often wrongly attributes these phenomena to import competition, disregarding the role of modern technology. What matters more is that the only type of lastingly growing economy is a market economy with a lot of competition, including that based on innovations. And market competition always produces some winners and some losers, at least in the relative sense (see the Schumpeterian "creative destruction"). Backlash against trade globalization is, therefore, just a manifestation of an old phenomenon—a protest against competition. In the Middle Ages, when the economy was shackled by monopolies, competition was morally condemned. The market revolution which started in the West in the early nineteenth century has changed this norm: the "creative destruction" due to market competition has stopped being perceived in general as morally reprehensible. Recent attacks against import competition and globalization resemble the old morality.

However, the most important observation regarding the negative outcomes ascribed, rightly or wrongly, to trade globalization is this: job losses related to competition in general (including trade globalization) depend not only on the extent of opening (Policy 1) but also on the institutions and policies which determine the adjustment, that is, the possibilities and incentives faced by the affected individuals to move to other occupations and/or to better locations (Policy 2). The intense competition, a basic determinant for long economic growth, combined with policies that limit individual adjustment, is bound to produce many more losers that the same competition coupled with a better institutional and policy environment for individual adjustment.

An economically and morally sensible conclusion is to improve Policies 2 instead of bashing import competition or other forms of market competition.

If the institutional environment for individual adjustment to increased import competition (and competition in general) is weak, there is a growing pressure on the part of the losers to limit competition, rather than to improve Policies 2. To what extent this pressure is translated into Policies 1 depends on the details of the political situation and on the kind of individuals operating in politics. It appears to me that the recent protectionist tendencies in the US, present among both the Republicans and the Democrats, are due to the fact that the people who perceive themselves as losers have had a strong presence in swing states. The increased political importance of the losers is not so typical of other democratic countries. But, of course, it is very unfortunate that such a situation has appeared in a country that is globally important and that used to be a global leader in external liberalization.

13.5 Financial Globalization

The number of fallacies in the discussion of financial globalization exceeds that regarding trade globalization, even though there are some common elements. Especially, (1) blaming both globalizations for the negative outcomes, which are caused, in fact, by wrong policies, and (2) disregarding the benefits from good globalization policies, that is, those that allow for external liberalization and the individuals' adjustment to new opportunities and threats.

Financial globalization is often associated with financial crises which, in turn, are blamed on market capitalism and especially on its financial sector. However, the deepest crises occur in the non-market regimes, which, by necessity, display a heavy concentration of political power (socialism). The reasons for this are clear: rulers without external constraints can launch and implement disastrous policies, almost totally crowding out legal markets (Fig. 13.6 and Table 13.1).

Therefore, the most important safeguard against the deepest crises consists in the division of powers within the society, which includes not only the checks and balances within the state but also private ownership and markets.

It is very superficial to blame the financial crises under capitalism on the markets. Contrary to the textbook presentation, these crises are not a phenomenon that occurs regularly across countries and time. The opposite is

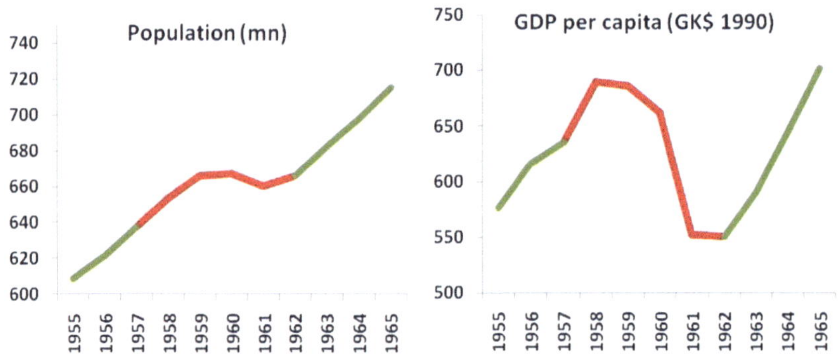

Fig. 13.6 The Great Leap Forward: population and GDP per capita, before and after. (*Source*: Maddison, Statistics on World Population, GDP and Per Capita GDP 1-2006AD). (Color figure online)

Table 13.1 The Great Leap Forward: growth rates, before and after

Growth rates								*Great Leap Forward*							
	1951	*1952*	*1953*	*1954*	*1955*	*1956*	*1957*	*1958*	*1959*	*1960*	*1961*	*1962*	*1963*	*1964*	*1965*
GDP	9.6%	9.5%	2.7%	0.9%	3.5%	6.9%	3.2%	8.6%	-0.6%	-3.5%	-16.5%	-0.4%	7.2%	9.2%	8.8%
Population	2%	2.1%	2.2%	2.4%	2.2%	2.1%	2.6%	2.5%	2%	0.2%	-1%	0.8%	2.5%	2.3%	2.4%

Source: Maddison, Statistics on World Population, GDP and Per Capita GDP 1-2006AD true: the incidence of financial crises has been very uneven, which strongly suggests that the differences in countries' policies are a deeper determinant of financial crisis (see Selgin 1997; Calomiris 1993). And such policies have been identified: they generally distort the behavior of the financial markets by encouraging excessive lending and borrowing, that is, fiscal and private credit booms. These policies include excessively low interest rates (due to interest rate subsidies or low central bank rates), "too big to fail" policy, tax regulations which favor borrowing relative to equity capital, overgenerous deposit insurance, and the like. Various combinations of these and other policies were also behind the recent global financial crisis (GFC).

A financial crisis becomes global when it includes a globally important economy, which nowadays is the US. However, even though the recent GFC is called "global," its impact has been far from uniform: certain countries were affected much more heavily (e.g. Spain, Ireland, and Greece) than others (e.g. Germany and Poland). The popular metaphors "contagion" and "domino effect" are misleading: countries' vulnerabilities to external financial shocks differ, and this depends again on their institutions and policies. One can distinguish two types of financial crisis, which take the form of the boom-bust episodes: the financial-fiscal and the fiscal-financial. In the former case, there is a real estate boom at the start which turns into the bust, causing a recession which spills over to public finance (the deficit explodes). Examples include Spain, Ireland, and the UK (Fig. 13.7 and Table 13.2).

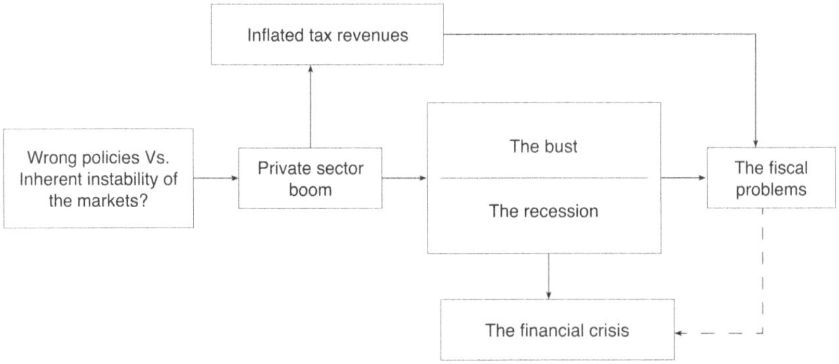

Fig. 13.7 The dynamics of the financial-fiscal crisis

Table 13.2 Household loans to GDP and Property Price Index for Spain, Ireland, and the UK

		2001	*2002*	*2003*	*2004*	*2005*	*2006*	*2007*	*2008*	*2009*	*2010*
Household loans to GDP	Ireland	49.62%	54.79%	62.59%	72.7%	85.99%	94.41%	101.7%	112.55%	123.28%	118.89%
	Spain	48.14%	52.08%	57.61%	64.41%	71.87%	79.22%	83.24%	83.92%	86.43%	85.69%
	UK	74.89%	76.15%	82.73%	87.53%	92.55%	98.34%	92.81%	84.45%	103.68%	99.16%
Property Price Index	Ireland	60.6	64.9	74.1	82.4	88.5	100.5	100	90.9	78.5	66.3
	Spain	47	54.4	64	75.2	85.6	94.6	100	100.7	93.2	89.6
	UK	50.3	63	72.8	82.9	85.6	93.5	100	85.3	88.1	88.6

Source: Eurostat; ECB; Nationwide

In the case of fiscal-financial crisis, at the beginning there is a fiscal boom which, when it bursts, spills over to the financial sector, that is, affects the banks which have financed the government borrowing spree. The best example here is Greece until 2010 (Fig. 13.8 and Table 13.3).

Even though the deeper causes of the financial crises include various faulty policies, one cannot deny that the risks of various disturbances in a financially interconnected world are higher than in a world where countries are financially isolated from each other. However, these risks have to be compared with the huge gains due to financial globalization, provided the right institutions and policies are in place.

Institutions in the host countries determine not only the amount of the incoming financial flows (Policy 1 in Fig. 13.1) but also their composition (Policy 2).

As noted in Sect. 13.1, FDI is, from the point of view of economic growth, the most important financial inflow because of its strong link to technology transfer. However, only some countries get large amounts of FDI: those with institutions and policies which respect private property rights and create a reasonable expectation that sudden policy reversals will be avoided. Very large economies like China can attract, for a certain time, large amounts of FDI even if these fundamentals are weak.

Some other financial inflows, for example, portfolio capital and international bank lending, are less strongly linked to the host country's economic growth. This is especially true if these inflows finance mortgage

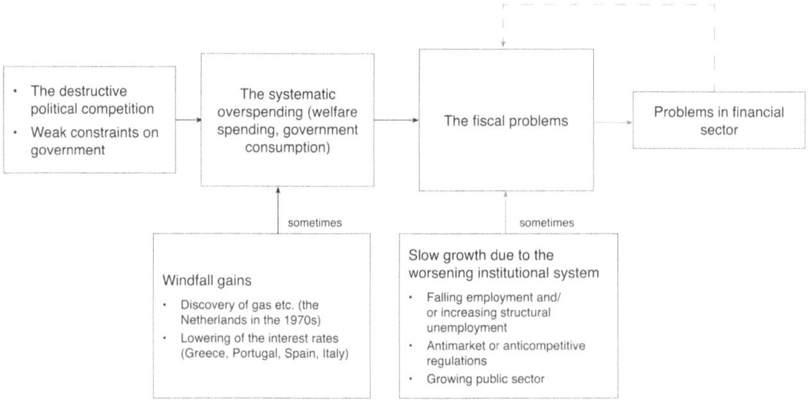

Fig. 13.8 The dynamics of fiscal-financial crisis

Table 13.3 General government total expenditure, general government net lending/borrowing, and general government net debt for Greece and Portugal

		1990	*1995*	*2000*	*2005*	*2006*	*2007*	*2008*	*2009*	*2010*
Greece	General government total expenditure	43.43	43.17	46.64	43.95	45.16	46.64	49.65	52.84	49.48
	General government net lending/borrowing	-14.51	-699	-3.69	-5.3	-6.12	-6.69	-9.8	-15.51	-10.42
	General government net debt	64.22	66.4	77.41	100.29	106.11	105.41	110.72	127.1	142.76
Portugal	General government total expenditure	39.26	39.66	39.29	42.42	40.82	44.3	44.64	49.83	50.64
	General government net lending/borrowing	-5.06	-3.41	-1.09	-2.54	-0.36	-3.15	-3.54	-10.11	-9.14
	General government net debt	n/a	n/a	41.97	57.95	58.77	63.66	67.36	78.79	88.7

Source: IMF

credit or fiscal booms. However, one should remember that these excesses are largely due to various combinations of bad policies rather than the inflows themselves.

13.6 Final Remarks

Let me finish with some observations and recommendations: the globalization process depends on the policies in the respective countries, especially for larger ones, and on other factors, especially on technical change. One should focus on policies so that they don't reverse the degree of countries' external opening and that their institutions allow for a better adjustment by individuals to new opportunities or threats. The globalization process may slow down if the technical change mutates the distribution of profitable locations of economic activity in the world, or because of the inevitable slowdown in China (Bordo 2017; Eichengreen 2016).

In discussing the outcomes ascribed to globalization one should distinguish the symptoms from the causes. Globalization is too often blamed for the results of bad policies, especially those which hamper individuals' adjustment to new pressures and those which encourage them to take excessive risks.

Crude anti-globalization, based on the nationalistic or utopian ethics, is very demagogic. However, it should not be neglected because the emotional irrationality appeals to many people and, therefore, can have dangerous political consequences.

In defending the achieved level of globalization one should appeal to its beneficiaries who would become losers if policies turn to trade protectionism, and this is especially relevant for the US. The European Union can and should play a central role in defending free trade in the world: at the same time, it should resist the protectionist pressures within its own Single Market.

References

Autor, David H., David Dorn, and Gordon H. Hanson. 2015. Untangling Trade and Technology: Evidence from Local Labour Markets. *The Economic Journal* (584): 621–646.

Balcerowicz, Leszek. 1995. *Socialism, Capitalism, Transformation*. Budapest: Central European University Press.

Baldwin, Richard. 2016. *The Great Convergence. Information technology and the New Globalization.* Cambridge, MA, and London: The Belknap Press and Harvard University Press.

Bordo, Michael D. 2017. The Second Era of Globalization is Not Yet Over: An Historical Perspective. Working Paper 319. Dallas: Federal Reserve Bank of Dallas Globalization and Monetary Policy Institute. Accessed June 5, 2020. https://www.dallasfed.org/~/media/documents/institute/wpapers/2017/0319.pdf.

Calomiris, Charles W. 1993. Financial Factors in the Great Depression. *Journal of Economic Perspectives* 7: 61–85.

Eichengreen, Barry. 2016. Will Globalisation Go into Reverse? *Prospect Magazine* 248. Accessed June 5, 2020. https://www.prospectmagazine.co.uk/magazine/will-globalisation-go-into-reverse-brexit-donald-trump.

Fajgelbaum, Pablo D., and Amit K. Khandelwal. 2016. Measuring the Unequal Gains from Trade. *The Quarterly Journal of Economics*, 131: 1113–1180. Accessed June 5, 2020. https://doi.org/10.1093/qje/qjw013.

Kazmin, Amy. 2014. India Risks Squandering Advantage as It Faces Urban Jobs Crunch. *Financial Times*, January 15. Accessed June 5, 2020. https://www.ft.com/content/80126cfe-7ce6-11e3-a579-00144feabdc0.

O'Rourke, Kevin H., Alan M. Taylor, and Jeffrey G. Williamson. 1996. Factor Price Convergence in the Late Nineteenth Century. *International Economic Review* 37: 499–530.

Selgin, George A. 1997. *Less than Zero. The Case for a Falling Price Level in a Growing Economy.* London: Institute of Economic Affairs.

Wolf, Martin. 2004. *Why Globalization Works.* New Haven: Yale University Press.

Wu, Harry X., and Conference Board China Center. 2014. China's Growth and Productivity Performance Debate Revisited—Accounting for China's Sources of Growth with a New Data Set. *Economics Program Working Paper Series* 14: 1–101. New York: The Conference Board. Accessed on June 29, 2020. https://www.conference-board.org/pdf_free/workingpapers/EPWP1401.pdf.

CHAPTER 14

The Great Recession and the Future of the EU

Edmond Alphandéry

As we are witnessing in Europe the unraveling of recent phenomena, such as the rise of populism and nationalism or the widening divide between different views on issues such as migration or the desirable degree of integration of the European Union (EU), it has become all the more clear that the power of ideas voiced through the channel of public opinion has a huge impact on the course of the European construction. This observation applies to the dynamic of the Economic and Monetary Union (EMU): a good illustration appears in the evolution of the eurozone in the aftermath of the great recession.

The traditional Anglo-Saxon analysis of the mechanisms inherent to the eurozone rests on the theory of optimum currency areas, which proper functioning implies integration of markets of goods and services, together with cross-border mobility of factors of production, labor and capital. Had this dominant doctrine prevailed in the 1990s when the EMU was launched, the euro would not have existed. There can be no doubt that

E. Alphandéry (✉)
Euro 50 Group, Former Minister of the Economy, Paris, France
e-mail: j.sarramalho@eaconseils.com

F. Giavazzi et al. (eds.), *The Liberal Heart of Europe*,
https://doi.org/10.1007/978-3-030-60368-7_14

the eurozone is not an optimum currency area. With hindsight however, it is worth examining how this currency which was created ex nihilo was able to work in spite of built-in weaknesses—which revealed themselves in broad daylight with the great recession—and why we have good reasons to hope that the euro is now on the right track.

I will start my analysis with this observation: a currency area can be viable over time even if it does not comply with the criteria of optimum currency areas. Italy before the euro, which was far from being an optimal currency area between North and South, is the most quoted case, but the *zone franc*, which has been de facto integrated to the eurozone since 1999, provides an even more telling example: the parity between the franc CFA and the euro is totally fixed, and its value has not changed since its devaluation in January 1994. No other currency area is more heterogeneous and distant from an optimum currency area than the *zone franc* in its relations with the eurozone. And yet countries of the *zone franc* remained unscathed by the great recession and its aftermath from which some European member states severely suffered. In fact, after the 1994 devaluation, macroeconomic imbalance procedures—similar to those put in place during the euro crisis—had been carried out and implemented by the French Treasury, which led these countries to abide by domestic and external disciplines that protected them from being engulfed into the euro crisis.

14.1 A Look Back at the Origins of the Euro Crisis

The facts and figures of the periods before, during and after the great recession show interesting features. During the first decade of the euro (1999–2008), the eurozone registered apparent "good" economic performance and the existing divergences did not comply with what one would have expected. Peripheral countries, Ireland, Greece—which entered the eurozone on January 1, 2001—and Spain, emerged as better performers than the three main economies: Germany, France and Italy (Fig. 14.1).

Similarly, the ratio of investment to GDP is better in Spain and Ireland than in France and Italy, while Germany is posting the lowest figure (Fig. 14.2).

During this period, the rate of employment also behaved rather well in peripheral countries: unemployment in Ireland remained low—the lowest

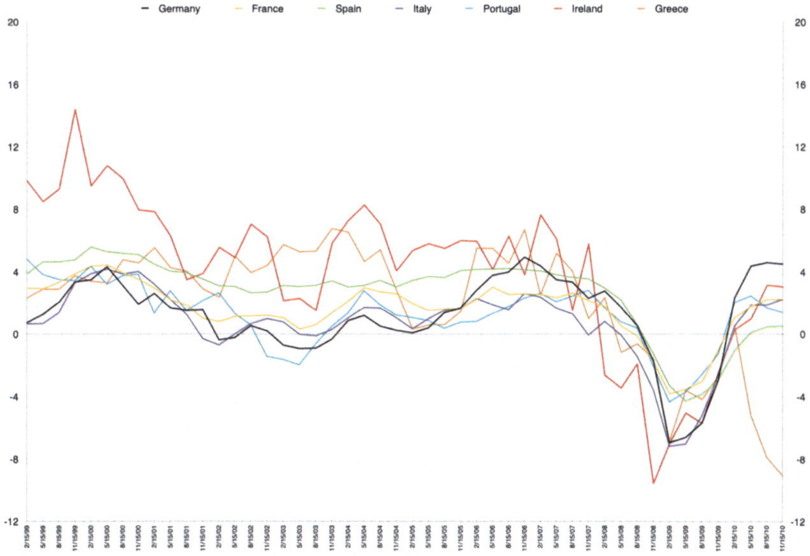

Fig. 14.1 Real growth of GDP (Y/Y as %) from 1999 to 2010: Germany, France, Spain, Italy, Portugal, Ireland and Greece. (*Source*: Datastream, Eurostat, NATIXIS)

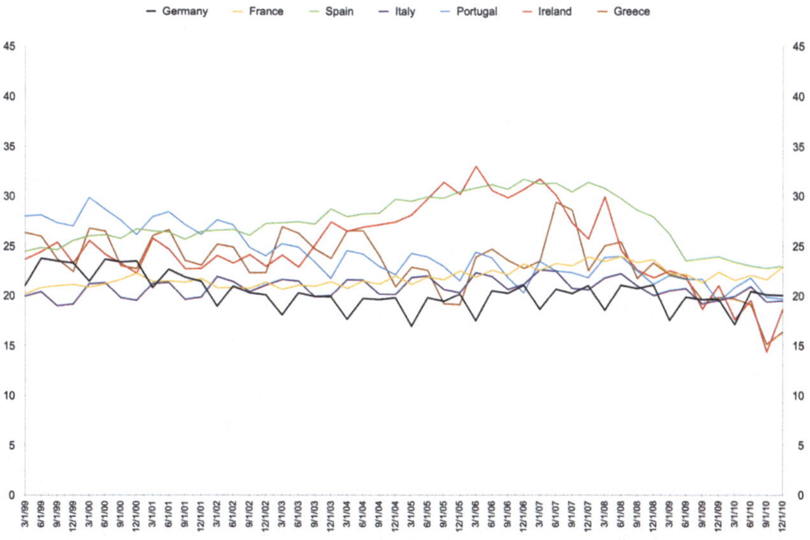

Fig. 14.2 Total investment (as % of nominal GDP) from 1999 to 2010: Germany, France, Spain, Italy, Portugal, Ireland and Greece. (*Source*: Eurostat, NATIXIS)

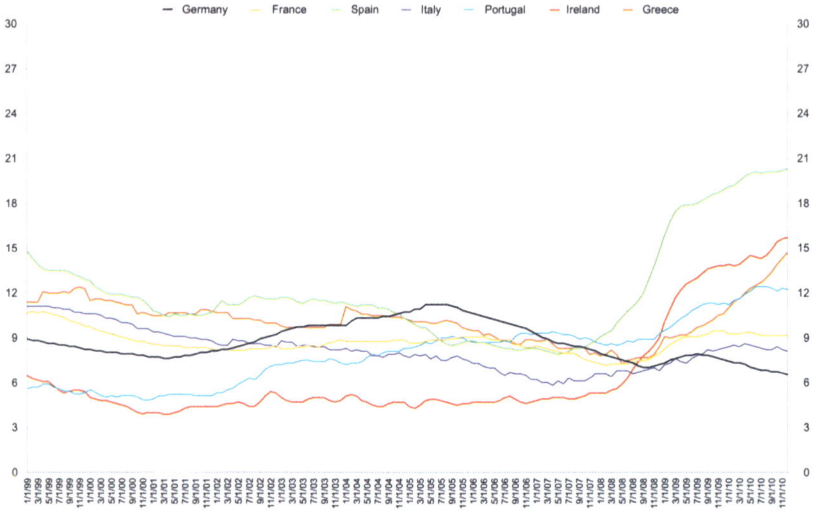

Fig. 14.3 Unemployment (in %) from 1999 to 2010: Germany, France, Spain, Italy, Portugal, Ireland and Greece. (*Source*: Datastream, Eurostat, NATIXIS)

rate—while Spain was the country where it decreased the most. Furthermore, Italy saw its rate of unemployment fall by nearly half from 1999 to 2009, and in Greece, it decreased from 11% in 2001, the year of its entry in the eurozone, to 8% in 2009. In contrast, Germany's rate of unemployment did not fall below 6% (Fig. 14.3).

Clearly, the euro acted as a catalyst for convergence to peripheral countries that were lagging behind before the introduction of the European currency. In 2008, before the burst of the Great Financial Crisis, the euro could be perceived as a boon in terms of performances as well as of convergence between member states. Nevertheless, we realized later on that policymakers had not paid enough attention to three weaknesses that surface from the data: (1) current-account imbalances, (2) surge in banks' credit and (3) build-up of excess confidence.

First is the state of current-account imbalances. During this period, in peripheral countries current-account deficits increased in Greece and Spain, remained large in Portugal and started to deepen in Ireland in 2005, up until the financial crisis. In the meantime, Germany was recording increasing surplus. Should we blame a country for accumulating deficit which is the consequence of its high economic growth and high level of investment (generating an excess aggregate demand)? In a full-fledged currency area such as the US, current-account imbalances between states do not matter since capital markets allow a permanent adjustment between investment and saving through cross-border financial flows. Such was the prevailing analysis among policymakers concerning the eurozone at that time. I remember visiting French Treasury officials in order to raise my concerns over the current-account deficit being the sign of a lack of competitiveness of the French economy, while the current account of the whole eurozone was regarded in fact as the relevant figure.

We have to concede though that better-integrated capital markets—as a result of the European currency—can in principle allow a member state to post a higher level of investment relative to its domestic saving. It risks nonetheless having to bear the painful adjustment set in motion to restore macroeconomic equilibrium in case of a loss of confidence, as it happens in any currency area which is ruled by the mechanisms of fixed exchange rates. In the case of the euro area, even if foreign exchange market between eurozone member states has de facto disappeared, loss of confidence in the stability of the macroeconomic equilibrium in any member state leads to an outflow of capital and therefore to a crisis on its financial market.

In member states where this imbalance had been fueled by high fiscal deficits such as Greece, Portugal or Italy, sovereign bond markets were the first targets under attack (Fig. 14.4).

The surge in banks' credit was the second weakness of this pre-financial crisis period: it led two peripheral countries, Ireland and Spain, to enter into dangerous mortgage bubbles. Even though these bubbles were part of a larger phenomenon (i.e. the "subprime crisis" in the US), one can hardly deny that with the EMU, the process of integration of capital markets contributed to their emergence through lower interest rates than would have prevailed, had the euro not existed (Fig. 14.5).

Last but not least, the build-up of excess confidence was a third feature of this pre-euro crisis period: with the emergence of the European currency, preexisting country risk premia started to crumble, leading to a dramatically rapid reduction of spreads in member states' interest rates and to their full convergence. As already noted, in a full-fledged currency area, this convergence is quite normal: it is the result of fully integrated capital markets. However, in the first decade of the euro, "homogeneous" perception of risks across member states did not correspond to the true risks which in fact were borne by investors. Some countries had too high levels

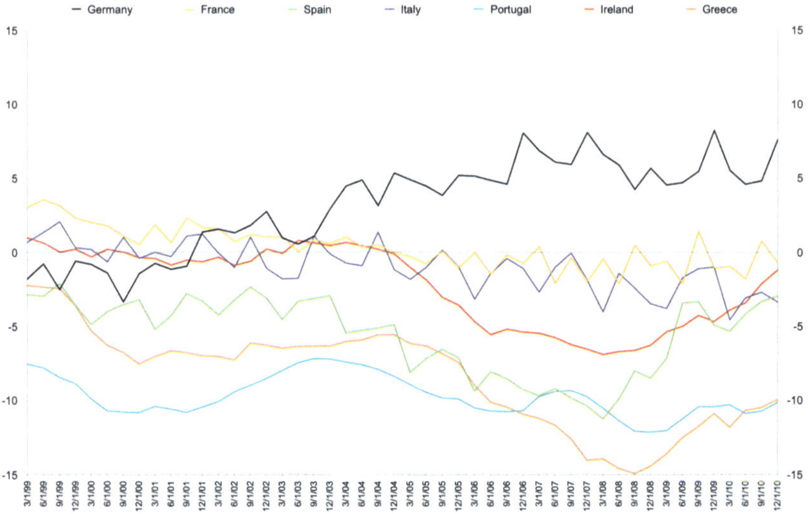

Fig. 14.4 Current-account balance (as % of nominal GDP) from 1999 to 2010: Germany, France, Spain, Italy, Portugal, Ireland and Greece. (*Source*: Datastream, NATIXIS)

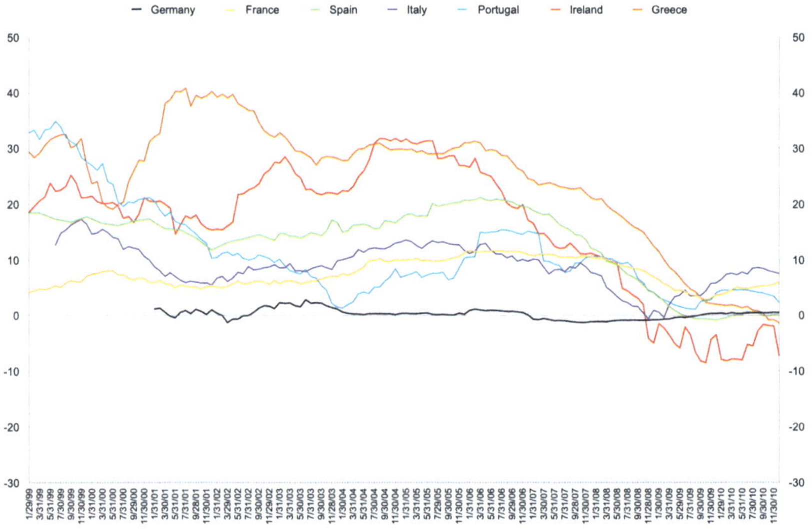

Fig. 14.5 Loans to households (Y/Y as %) from 1999 to 2010. (*Source*: Datastream, Central Banks, NATIXIS)

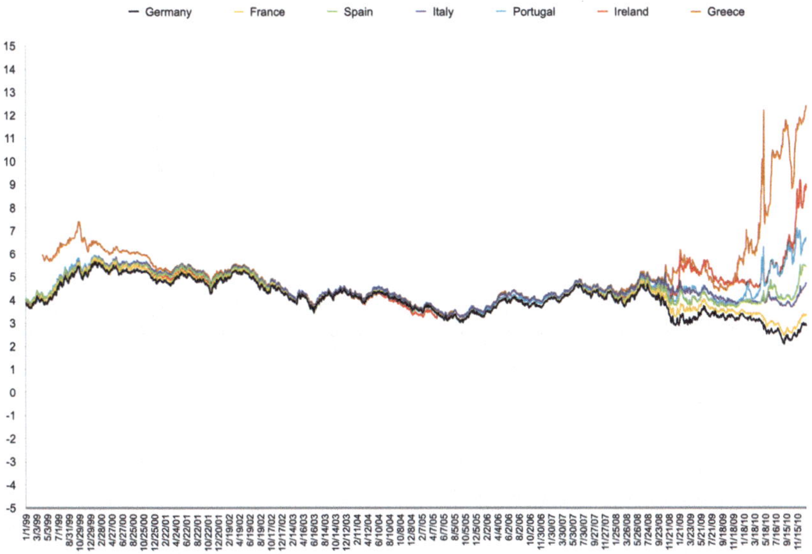

Fig. 14.6 Interest rate on ten-year government bonds (as %) from 1999 to 2010. (*Source*: Datastream, NATIXIS)

of debt (Italy, Greece), in others either fiscal deficits were much higher than the average or banks' credits had dangerously increased (Spain, Ireland). In addition to that, most peripheral countries were also posting high and rising current-account deficits (Fig. 14.4). Such a convergence in interest rates was hardly sustainable: any external shock capable of drawing investors' attention to excess of confidence in a member state's financial equilibrium could put its financial market into trouble: this is precisely exactly what happened in the aftermath of the Great Financial Crisis (Fig. 14.6).

14.2 The Great Recession, EMU and the Power of Ideas

The great recession triggered a triple asymmetric shock on the eurozone: on real economies, on fiscal stances and on financial assets, sovereign bonds in the first place. Concerning the evolution of real growth of GDP (Fig. 14.1), the trough's magnitude in 2009 varied from -4% to -10%, without any divide between peripheral countries and core countries: Ireland was the most affected, while Spain and even Greece had to bear a less painful stroke. The German economy was unexpectedly severely hit. Asymmetry of the shock's impact appears more clearly in the aftermath of the great recession: Greece fell into a severe and protracted contraction of its economy no later than 2010. The Irish economy started to recover that very same year, to become the success story of the eurozone's return to economic growth after 2013. In this process, Spain's rebound was second to Ireland, while France and—even worse—Italy were lagging behind. These disparities come out of discrepancies in terms of resilience as well as (we will see later) of member states' reactions to the crisis.

The second shock out of the great recession was borne by member states' finances. According to the motto coming from the International Monetary Fund (IMF), as well as from many pundits and policymakers, countries should increase their public spending in order to avert the risk of falling into full depression (Fig. 14.7).

Member states responded with more or less enthusiasm (Table 14.1): fiscal impulse was more pronounced in France and Spain than in Germany and Italy burdened by a high level of public debt.

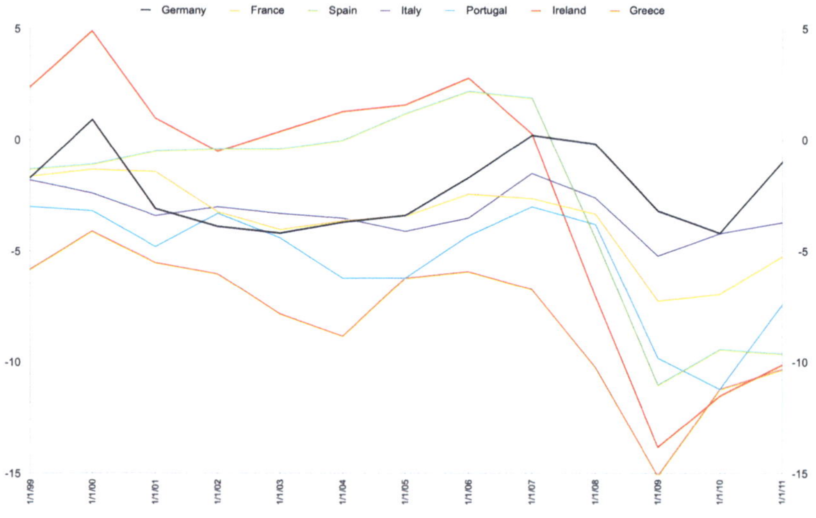

Fig. 14.7 Fiscal deficit (as % of nominal GDP) from 1999 to 2010. (*Source*: Datastream, Forecasts NATIXIS)

Table 14.1 Assessment of the fiscal policy stance according to different entities (percentage points of potential GDP)

	2008–2010	*2011–2015*	*2016–2017*	*2008–2017*	*Potential growth (2008–2017)*
Germany					
IMF	1.7	-2.0	0.5	**0.2**	1.3
OECD	1.5	-1.5	0.5	**0.5**	1.2
OFCE	2.0	-2.0	1.1	**1.2**	1.4
Spain					
IMF	6.6	-7.2	0.5	**-0.2**	1.0
OECD	5.2	-6.9	1.5	**-0.2**	1.0
OFCE	7.4	-8.4	0.1	**-0.9**	1.0
France					
IMF	2.2	-3.2	0.1	**-0.9**	1.0
OECD	1.7	-2.8	-0.5	**-1.6**	1.1
OFCE	3.1	-4.5	-0.1	**-1.5**	1.3
Italy					
IMF	1.1	-2.7	0.8	**-0.8**	-0.1
OECD	0.7	-2.6	1.5	**-0.5**	-0.1
OFCE	1.2	-3.6	0.5	**-1.8**	-0.3
UK					
IMF	1.3	-1.7	-1.6	**-2.0**	1.3
OECD	1.5	-1.4	-2.7	**-2.6**	1.3
OFCE	3.9	-3.3	-2.3	**-1.7**	1.6
US					
IMF	5.5	-5.9	0.9	**0.5**	1.6
OECD	4.5	-5.7	0.2	**-0.9**	1.7
OFCE	7.1	-6.5	0.6	**1.2**	1.5

Sources: IMF (World Economic Outlook, October 2017), OECD Economic Outlook (November 2017), Calculation by Observatoire Français des Conjonctures Economiques (OFCE)

With the deepening of the euro crisis, the introduction by European authorities of a more compelling fiscal framework led to an abrupt turnaround in member states' "fiscal stances" which became contractionary (Table 14.1). At the same time the monetary policy of the European Central Bank (ECB), after the launch of a second wave of quantitative easing (QE) by the US Federal Reserve (the Fed) in 2010, appeared as being relatively too restrictive. The ensuing outflow of capital from the euro area strengthened the value of the European currency, which reached a higher level than it would have been in the absence of this Fed's QE. In the context of the euro crisis, while many economies were fragile, the "policy

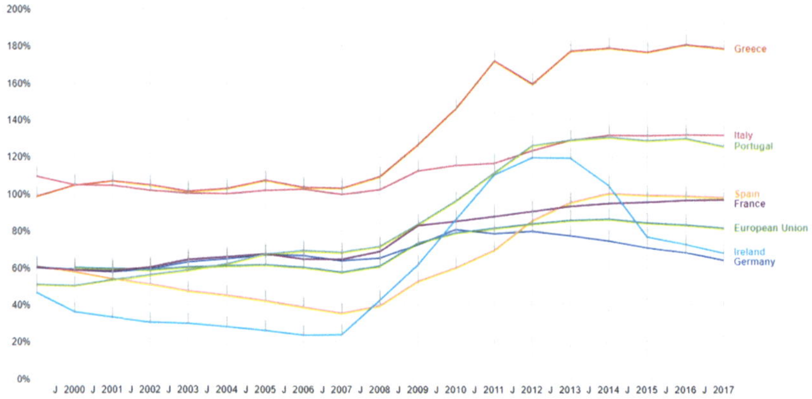

Fig. 14.8 Government debt (as % of GDP) from 1999 to 2017. (*Source*: Eurostat)

mix" of the eurozone in its fiscal and monetary dimensions, far from being anticyclical as it should have been, became procyclical.

Lastly, what I would call an asymmetric "shock of confidence" hit the financial markets. In the aftermath of the great recession and in the wake of the euro crisis, spreads between member states' interest rates began to widen; country risk premia reappeared. Due to a loss of confidence in its fiscal policy, Greece registered the largest spread increase. Severely hit by these shocks, most peripheral countries entered into crises fueled by outflows of capital from the periphery to the core of the eurozone (Fig. 14.8).

To address this turmoil, the ECB reshaped its monetary policy in three steps: the famous "whatever it takes" of Mario Draghi, the creation of a new instrument (the so-called Outright Monetary Transactions) and the launch of QE in March 2015. Monetary policy from procyclical became anticyclical (Fig. 14.9).

On the fiscal side, European authorities responded by setting up the "economic semester" and also by the "macroeconomic imbalance procedure": two major steps toward better coordination and convergence of economic policies of member states. Furthermore, the euro crisis led to more solidarity among member states, a major dimension of any currency area: the European Financial Stabilization Mechanism (EFSM) followed by the European Stability Mechanism (ESM) was created in order to help countries in trouble under conditionalities.

Fig. 14.9 Euro/dollar exchange rate (1999–2018). (*Source*: Tradingeconomics.com, OTC Interbank)

Jean Monnet famously said that "Europe will be forged in crises, and will be the sum of the solutions adopted to solve these crises": this shock, which violence was unmatched in the history of the European construction, worked as an incentive for Europe to move forward and progress. Debate on these new orientations which at its origin had been essentially technocratic became a source of political bickering. Opposition came not only from the Euroskeptics but even from the pro-European camp.

I will illustrate the impact of the power of ideas on the fate of the European currency through the events that unfolded in Greece, France and Italy at the end of the euro crisis and thereafter in the years 2015–2017.

In Greece in January 2015, the radical left party "Syriza" won the parliamentary elections. On June 30, the country defaulted to the IMF. Prime Minister Tsipras decided to call for a referendum to reject the deal with creditors. The ensuing "no" vote led to a major liquidity crisis. Tsipras had then the choice between sticking to his ideological position which would have ended with Greece leaving the eurozone (as proposed by his finance minister), or changing foot by making an economic and financial U-turn. He had to take into account the fact that the majority of the Greek people wanted to keep the euro and, hence, in a few days, the decision (taken reluctantly) to act in conformity with creditors' demands and to abide by the discipline and rules of the European Union.

The French presidential election of May 2017 gives another illustration of people's attachment to the European project. At that time there was a large concern of a possible Marine Le Pen's victory, and hence of a risk of France exiting the euro (the pillar of her platform). This led to fears of a major crisis, with the potential to threaten the existence of the European currency itself. Just before the first round of the presidential election, I entered the fray, although modestly, by publishing an op-ed in *Le Figaro* titled "The Euro Exit: A Foolishness." A press campaign ensued. In the famous TV debate when Emmanuel Macron attacked her on the euro, she proved weak and confused. The French concluded that an exit from the euro would lead to chaos. It resulted not only in Le Pen's defeat but also—even more strikingly—in the "Front National" dropping the exit of the euro out of its political platform.

I end with Italy: it is interesting to observe that after the French election, the two populist and fundamentally Euroskeptic movements preferred to avoid campaigning on leaving the euro. Furthermore, when the League and the Five-Star Movement presented a government with a notoriously anti-euro finance minister, they were confronted with a veto from the president of the republic and forced to accept finance and foreign ministers who were pro-Europeans. Once again, the political checks and balances played in favor of the euro, because the Italian people were aware that the economic and social price to be paid for leaving the European currency would be huge and that at the end of the day the place of Italy was to be in the European Union.

Index[1]

[1] Note: Page numbers followed by 'n' refer to notes.

F. Giavazzi et al. (eds.), *The Liberal Heart of Europe*,
https://doi.org/10.1007/978-3-030-60368-7

The manufacturer's authorised representative in the EU is Springer Nature Customer Service Centre GmbH, Europaplatz 3, 69115 Heidelberg, Germany. If you have any concerns regarding our products, please contact ProductSafety@springernature.com

Printed and bound by CPI Group (UK) Ltd, Croydon, CR0 4YY

30/09/2026

02225700-0002